Living in the Alps

WOHNEN IN DEN ALPEN

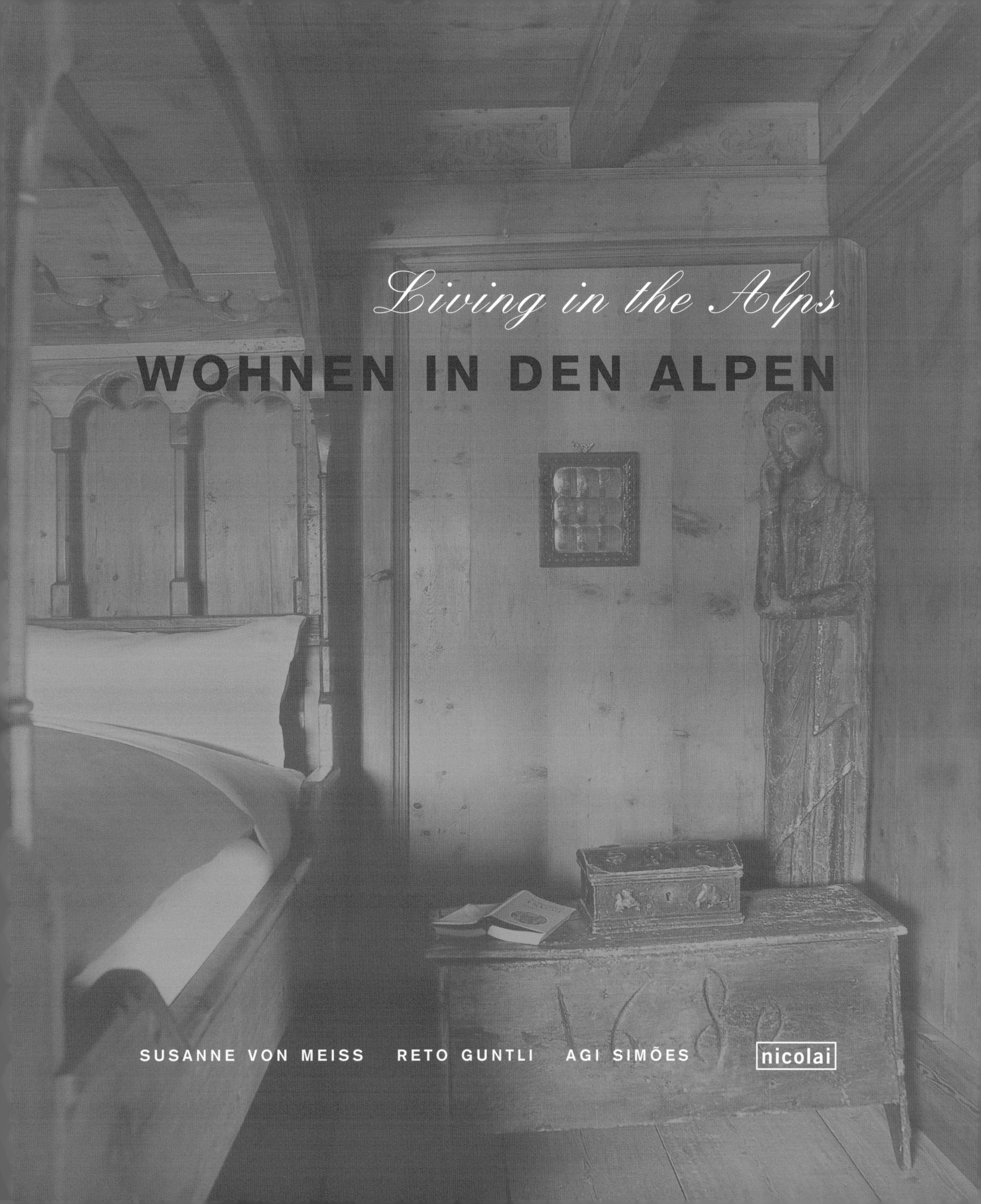

Living in the Alps

WOHNEN IN DEN ALPEN

SUSANNE VON MEISS   RETO GUNTLI   AGI SIMÕES

nicolai

Mad about wood Holzrausch

A strong link

This is exactly the harassed city-dweller's idea of a garden of Eden in the Swiss Alpine region: in summer, nothing but rich green meadows as far as the eye can see, with innumerable cows trotting in a leisurely manner around an old wooden house, to the cheerful tinkle of cowbells. And in winter, the most wonderful skiing piste right outside the door. Here, up in the Bernese mountains a little above the community of Saanen, lies a secluded and idyllic valley. And here, too, is the winter mecca (and summer oasis!) of Sophie and Jacques Prézioso: the almost-four-hundred-year-old, lovingly converted and immensely cosy chalet called "Charlix". In 1607, during the religious conflicts of the Reformation, a well-respected Catholic from Saanen had retreated to the little valley and built this house with his own hands, the first in the whole area. "It was love at first sight," says the French owner, Sophie Prézioso, with a sparkle in her eye; she likes to call it a *coup de foudre*. Sophie and her husband Jacques, with their children Charles and Alix and the two English bulldogs Max and Ingrid, had been on a walking tour in this remote valley when they came across the little "for sale" sign. "Out of curiosity, we had a look at the delightful wooden house – and we were totally captivated." They bought the old chalet on the spot – and this despite the fact that they had had no intention whatsoever of buying a holiday home. "But this house is not just a house, it is absolutely unique," continues Sophie Prézioso enthusiastically. "It's a strong house, one with character, one that just doesn't ever let you go." The chalet "Charlix" (the name combining those of the two children) has seen very little change in the last four hundred years. The outer corridors have been walled up, and an extension at the back has created more space. Since the house is under a preservation order, and is considered a significant architectural feature of the area, the impressive front façade has remained untouched. "In order to restore the original inscription – the date and an image of Christ and the Virgin Mary – we had to obtain permission from Berne," recalls Sophie Prézioso, who for months regularly drove up from her home in Geneva to the valley, to supervise the necessary work on the newly acquired chalet. Although the new owners tried to preserve as much as possible of the old fabric, some alterations were necessary in the interior of the house. After all, even in 1994, when they bought the house, there was neither heating nor an electricity supply in this remote mountain paradise! And so the new bathrooms, too, were lovingly integrated into the extension with hundred-year-old wooden planks. The kitchen, with the beautiful inlaid floor found by the owners at the flea market "Marché Paul-Bert" in Paris, was installed in the former stable. "The house speaks a language of its own," Sophie Prézioso explains. "It has its own temperament, and you can't try to contradict it or to force anything on it." And so, in the course of their conversion work, the happy Préziosos allowed themselves to be led by it to a great extent. The result is enchanting: a great deal of old wood, many simple antique deco-

Top: Wood, stone and leather: a perfect combination even for the English bulldogs Ingrid and Max. **Oben: Holz, Stein und Leder: eine perfekte Kombination, auch für die englischen Bulldoggen Ingrid und Max.**

Far left: Every detail fits: a chamois horn object over an old sofa in the living room. **Links außen: Jedes Detail stimmt: Gamshornobjekt über einem alten Sofa im Wohnzimmer.**

Left: The Prézioso family's chalet "Charlix" dates from the year 1607. **Links: Aus dem Jahr 1607 stammt das Chalet „Charlix" der Familie Prézioso.**

rative objects, simple checked, striped or monochrome fabrics, and a surprising degree of perfectly disguised comfort. Some of the old simple peasant furniture was already in the house when Sophie and Jacques bought it, and so the couple went in search of additional objects, small items of furniture, offbeat things that would fit well into this mountain home of four hundred square metres with its very individual character. The chalet "Charlix" has six medium-sized rooms – and a seventh, an enormous one, that serves as a TV room, a nursery and a room for all purposes. Charles and Alix's room is a child's dream come true, for it can be reached only by means of a wooden ladder, lying directly under the roof. Anyone who, like Sophie and Jacques, loves country life, fishing, golf, driving or cycling, who enjoys do-it-yourself and has an eye for unusual objects, ought to look out for a solitary valley – who knows, perhaps there will be a little sign saying "for sale".

Eine starke Verbindung

Genauso stellt sich der gehetzte Großstädter den Garten Eden im helvetischen Alpenland vor: im Sommer nur satte grüne Weiden, soweit das Auge reicht; dazu unzählige Kühe, die zum fröhlich wilden Glockengebimmel gemächlich um ein altes Holzhaus trotten. Und im Winter die herrlichste Skipiste direkt vor der Haustür. Hier oben in den Berner Bergen etwas oberhalb der Gemeinde Saanen liegt ein abgeschiedenes und verträumtes Tal. Und hier befindet sich auch das Wintermekka (und die Sommeroase!) von Sophie und Jacques Prézioso: das beinahe vierhundert Jahre alte, liebevoll umgebaute und urgemütliche Chalet „Charlix". Im Jahr 1607, während der Zeit der Reformation mit ihren religiösen Wirren, hatte sich ein angesehener Katholik aus Saanen in das kleine Tal zurückgezogen und dieses Haus, das allererste in der Gegend überhaupt, mit seinen eigenen Händen errichtet. „Es war Liebe auf den ersten Blick", erzählt die französische Besitzerin Sophie Prézioso mit einem Blitzen in den Augen; sie nennt es gerne einen „coup de foudre". Mit ihrem Ehemann Jacques, den Kindern Charles und Alix sowie den beiden englischen Bulldogen Max und Ingrid waren sie zu Fuß in diesem abgelegenen Tal unterwegs, als sie auf die kleine Verkaufstafel stießen. „Aus Neugier haben wir uns das entzückende Holzhaus angeschaut – und waren völlig hingerissen." Sie kauften das Chalet auf der Stelle – und dies, obwohl sie überhaupt kein Ferienhaus haben wollten. „Doch dieses Haus ist nicht einfach ein Haus, es ist absolut einmalig", fährt Sophie Prézioso mit Enthusiasmus fort, „es ist ein starkes Haus, eines mit Charakter, eines, das dich gar nie mehr los lässt." Das Chalet „Charlix" (zusammengezogen aus den beiden Kindernamen) hat sich in den letzten vierhundert Jahren nur wenig verändert: Die Außengänge wurden zugemauert, und ein Anbau an der Hinterseite hat mehr Platz geschaffen. Da das Haus unter Denkmalschutz steht und als bedeutendes Architekturzeugnis dieser Gegend gilt, ist auch die eindrückliche Frontfassade unbeschadet geblieben. „Um die Beschriftung – Jahreszahl, Christus und Mutter Gottes – wieder hervorzuholen, mussten wir von Bern eine Genehmigung einholen", erinnert sich Sophie Prézioso, die über Monate hinweg regelmäßig von ihrem Wohnort Genf ins Bergtal hinaufgefahren ist, um die notwendigen Arbeiten im frisch erworbenen Chalet zu überwachen. Auch wenn die neuen Bewohner versuchten, so viel wie möglich von der alten Substanz zu bewahren, so waren im Innern des Hauses doch einige Veränderungen nötig. Schließlich gab es noch im Verkaufsjahr 1994 weder Heizung noch elektrischen Strom in diesem einsam gelegenen Bergparadies! Und so wurden auch die neuen Badezimmer liebevoll mit hundert Jahre alten Holzbrettern in den Anbau integriert. Die Küche mit dem wunderschönen eingelegten Boden, den das Besitzerpaar auf dem Flohmarkt „Marché Paul-Bert" in Paris gefunden hat, setzte man in den ehemaligen Stall. „Das Haus spricht eine eigene Sprache", erklärt Sophie Prézioso, „es hat sein eigenes Temperament, da muss man weder versuchen zu widersprechen noch irgend etwas zu erzwingen." Und so haben sich die glücklichen Préziosos bei ihrer

The nursery is furnished in the style of Ralph Lauren. ***Im Stil von Ralph Lauren ist das Kinderzimmer eingerichtet.***

Umbauarbeit weitgehend davon leiten lassen. Das Resultat ist bestechend: viel altes Holz, viele antike einfache Dekorationsgegenstände, simple karierte, gestreifte oder uni farbige Stoffe und überraschend viel perfekt versteckter Komfort. Einige der alten einfachen Bauernmöbel waren bereits im Haus, als Sophie und Jacques es übernahmen, und so gingen die beiden auf die Suche nach zusätzlichen Objekten, kleinen Möbeln, ausgefallenen Dingen, die in dieses vierhundert Quadratmeter große Bergdomizil mit seinem ureigenen Charakter passen würden. Sechs nicht allzu große Zimmer besitzt das Chalet „Charlix" – und ein siebtes, ein riesiges, das sowohl als TV-Room, als Kinderspielzimmer oder Zimmer-für-alle-Fälle dient. Das Reich von Charles und Alix ist ein Kindertraum für sich, denn es ist nur über eine Holzleiter zu erreichen, da es direkt unter dem Dach liegt. Wer wie Sophie und Jacques das Landleben liebt, wer gerne fischt, Golf spielt, Motor- oder Fahrrad fährt, wer gerne bastelt und ein Auge für besondere Objekte hat, wer gerne Ski fährt, „und zwar jedes Wochenende, wann immer wir können", der sollte nach einem einsamen Tal Ausschau halten ... wer weiß, vielleicht steht da eine kleine Verkaufstafel.

Not one piece too many: an antique long table with matching chairs. ***Kein Stück zu viel: ein antiker langer Tisch mit passenden Stühlen.***

Page 12: Black and white checks in the entrance form the background for a Biedermeier chair and a coat-stand made from a stag's antlers. ***Seite 12: Schwarz-weißes Karo im Eingang bildet den Hintergrund für einen Biedermeierstuhl und ein Hirschgeweihständer.***

Page 13: A skilful pairing: a rustic rocking-chair with a horn seat in the entrance hall. ***Seite 13: Geschickt gepaart: rustikaler Schaukelstuhl mit Hornsessel im Entree.***

Breakfast in the former xowshed. The floor tiles are one hundred years old. ***Frühstück im ehemaligen Kuhstall. Die Kacheln am Boden sind hundert Jahre alt.***

Brown wood and white piqué dominate in the guestroom. ***Braunes Holz und weißes Pikee dominieren im Gästezimmer.***

In Würde gealtert

Die Sonne scheint aus einem Wolkenkranz herab, zwischen Palmenzweigen spielen kleine Engel auf ihren Posaunen, und unzählige Sterne leuchten aus dem graublauen Himmel. Die bemalte Decke des urgemütlichen Wohnzimmers im „Chalet an der Matte“ im Saanenland ist ein Kunstwerk für sich. “Als meine Eltern das alte Holzhaus vor über fünfzig Jahren auf einer Wanderung entdeckten, war es völlig verlottert“, berichtet der heutige Hausherr, „das Wohnzimmer befand sich einen Meter tiefer unten, die schöne Decke war übermalt und die Fenster eingeschlagen; neben der Stube gab es eine verlassene Werkstatt und eine kleine Rauchküche mit einem offenen Kamin. Im oberen Stock wurde neben dem Heuboden gesponnen und gewoben.“ Zehn Jahre lang hatte das Bauernhaus leer gestanden, und so brauchte es eine gehörige Portion Phantasie, um sich das Innenleben des über fünfhundert Jahre alten Hauses vorzustellen. Die neuen Besitzer besaßen diese Gabe: Sie ließen Decke und Wände ablaugen, die alten Fenster restaurieren, eine Bibliothek in die Werkstatt einbauen und die offene Raumküche zu einem urigen Entree umfunktionieren. Ein Teil des Raums über dem Stall auf dem Heuboden wurde zu einem schmalen, langen und mit Fichtenholz ausgelegten Badezimmer ausgebaut. Eingerichtet ist das „Chalet an der Matte“ – Matte bedeutet Wiese – schlicht und einfach mit Holzmöbeln aus dem siebzehnten und achtzehnten Jahrhundert. Aus dem Elsass, dem Schwarzwald und aus der Schweiz kommen die eleganten schwarz-weißen Porzellanteller, -tassen und -krüge, die der Hausherr mit Leidenschaft sammelt. Er findet, „dass sie perfekt auf die antike hölzerne Anrichte aus dem Bündnerland passen“. Und ins älteste Holzhaus im Saanenland.

***Oben links:** Das älteste Haus im Saanenland: das über fünfhundert Jahre alte „Chalet an der Matte“.* *Top left: The oldest house in the Saanenland: the “Chalet an der Matte”, more than five hundred years old.*

***Oben rechts:** Verblasst, aber noch erkennbar: das alte Deckengemälde in der Holzstube.* *Top right: Faded but still recognizable: the old ceiling painting in the wood-panelled living room.*

***Rechts:** „Rauchige“ Patina: Der Vorraum zur Stube war einst eine Rauchküche mit offenem Feuer.* *Right: “Smoky” patina: the anteroom to the living room was once a smokehouse with an open fire.*

Aged with dignity

The sun shines down through a wreath of clouds, and between palm branches little angels play their trumpets, while countless stars shine from the grey-blue sky. The painted ceiling of the cosy living room in the "Chalet an der Matte" in the Saanenland is a work of art in itself. "When my parents found this old wooden house more than fifty years ago while on a walking tour," the present owner reports, "it was totally run-down. The living-room area was a metre deeper, the beautiful ceiling was overpainted and the windows broken; next door to the front room was a disused workshop, and a little kitchen with an open fireplace." For ten years the farmhouse had stood empty, and it took a good measure of imagination to picture the interior life of the more than five-hundred-year-old house. The new owners had this gift. They had the ceilings and walls washed, the old windows restored, a library was built into the workshop, and the old open kitchen was transformed into a welcoming entrance hall. Part of the space above the stable in the hayloft was extended to form a long, narrow bathroom panelled with sprucewood. The "Chalet an der Matte" ("Matte" means meadow) is furnished simply and unpretentiously with wooden furniture of the seventeenth and eighteenth centuries. From Alsace, the Black Forest and Switzerland come the black and white china plates, cups and jugs of which the master of the house is a passionate collector. He finds "that they go perfectly with the antique wooden sideboard from the Grisons". And with the oldest wooden house in the Saanenland.

Links: Zwischen den Treppen öffnet sich die Tür zu den Kellerräumen. *Left: Between the staircases the door opens to the cellar space.*

Heute befindet sich der Haupteingang auf der überdachten Seite des alten Chalets. *Today the main entrance is on the roofed side of the old chalet.*

Winterfest Winter-proof

Make us something cosy, something colourful, something un-Swiss," was the request of the owners of the little old apartment in the mountain resort of Klosters in the Grisons to their friend Countess Monika Apponyi. The Austrian-born interior designer, living in London, is known for her unusual combinations of different decorative styles, and she created for her friends exactly what they wanted: a little jewel-box in the most brilliant colours. From the narrow passageway, which is covered in a simple caramel-beige checked pattern, and bathed in muted light from an antlered chandelier, plain wooden doors lead into the three bedrooms. Burgundy Ralph Lauren patterns and dark-stained wood give the first and smallest bedroom a cave-like atmosphere. Pale green toile de Jouy on the walls of the middle bedroom, on the other hand, gives it a fresh rural character, and a Swedish-inspired beige and pale blue for the nursery adds gaiety to the almost one-hundred-year-old house in the very centre of the village. The tapering room directly next to the living room has a splendid view of the ski mountain Gotschna, but before the renovation it was lacking in charm and distinction. Monika Apponyi found a simple solution to this problem. She adopted an idea that is often realized in more southern latitudes: all the walls of the small room were bathed in a dark, slightly shimmering red by her favourite painter, Paul MacDonnell, as was the newly made wooden framework on the floor, which was transformed with the help of two thick, striped mattresses and a number of red cushions into a sumptuous oriental divan. "And to integrate this 'Moroccan room'," as the owners like to call it today, "into the wood-panelled salon, a local joiner constructed a wide folding door as a connecting entrance, which Paul painted in 'wood'," explains the designer. Thus the two small rooms, furnished with kilim rugs, became a spacious and comfortable living room with both Arabic and Swiss elements. For the heart of this attractive holiday home – the kitchen-cum-living room – the colour theme was "yellow ochre and Chinese red": handmade tiles from Portugal for the wall above the kitchen area, antique brown and white china plates from Ireland for the walls, a black and white linoleum floor from England, and furniture from Thailand, India and Switzerland vividly demonstrate that the standard Swiss style is not required in this mountain home.

Mach uns etwas Gemütliches, etwas Farbiges, etwas Unschweizerisches", baten die Besitzer der kleinen alten Dachwohnung im Graubündnerischen Bergort Klosters ihre Freundin Gräfin Monika Apponyi. Und da die in London wohnhafte österreichische Interior-Designerin bekannt ist für ihre ungewöhnlichen Verbindungen verschiedener Einrichtungsstile, hat sie ihren Freunden genau das kreiert, was sich diese gewünscht haben: eine kleine Schmuckschatulle in den leuchtendsten Farben. Vom schmalen Gang, der in einem schlichten karamel-beigen Karostoff gehalten ist und von einem Hirschgeweihleuchter in gedämpftes Licht getaucht wird, führen einfache Holztüren in die drei Schlafzimmer. Burgunderfarbene Ralph Lauren-Muster und dunkel gebeiztes Holz geben dem ersten, dem kleinsten, Schlafraum ein höhlenartiges Ambiente. Hellgrünes toile de Jouy-Tuch an den Wänden verleiht dem mittleren dagegen einen ländlich frischen Charakter, und ein schwedisch inspiriertes Beige-Hellblau fürs Kinderzimmer bringt Fröhlichkeit unter das Dach des fast hundert Jahre alten Hauses mitten im Dorfzentrum. Dem abgeschrägten Raum direkt neben dem Wohnzimmer mit herrlichem Blick auf den Skiberg „Gotschna" fehlte es vor der Renovierung an Charme und Caché. Für dieses Problem fand Monika Apponyi eine simple Lösung. Sie griff eine Idee auf, die in südlicheren Breitengraden häufig umgesetzt wird: Sie ließ sämtliche Wände des kleinen Zimmers von dem von ihr bevorzugten Maler Paul MacDonnell in ein dunkles, leicht schillerndes Rot tauchen, genauso wie das neu gezimmerte Holzgestell am Boden, das mit Hilfe von zwei dicken gestreiften Matratzen und vielen roten Kissen in einen üppigen orientalischen Diwan verwandelt wurde. „Und um dieses marokkanische Zimmer", wie es die Besitzer heute gerne nennen, „in den holzgetäfelten Salon zu integrieren, fertigte

In defiance of rainy autumn days: the kitchen-cum-living-room in brilliant yellow and red.
Im Kampf gegen regnerische Herbsttage: Die Wohnküche in leuchtend gelb und rot.

ein lokaler Schreiner eine breite Falttüre – von Paul in ‚Holz' gemalt – als Durchgangstor", erklärt die Designerin. So ist aus den beiden kleinen, mit Kelimteppichen ausgelegten Zimmern ein großzügiger, behaglicher Wohnraum mit arabisch-helvetischen Elementen geworden.Für das Herz dieses schmucken Feriendomizils – die Wohnküche – hieß das Farbenmotto „ockergelb und chinarot": Handgefertigte Kacheln aus Portugal für das Mauerstück über der Küchenstrecke, antike braun-weiße Porzellanplatten aus Irland für die Wände, ein schwarz-weißer Linoleumboden aus England und Möbel aus Thailand, Indien und der Schweiz demonstrieren es augenfällig: Helvetischer Einheitsstil ist in dieser Bergwohnung nicht gefragt.

Top left: Here, lighter colours were chosen: the nursery, in grey and beige with a painted screen from the flea market. ***Oben links: Hier fiel die Wahl auf hellere Farben: das Kinderzimmer in grau und beige mit einem bemalten Paravent vom Flohmarkt.***

Top right: View from the living room into the corridor. ***Oben rechts: Blick vom Wohnzimmer in den Korridor.***

Furnishing fabric by Ralph Lauren.
Stoffbespannung von Ralph Lauren.

Wallpapaer in small checks adorns the entrance to this mountain abode. ***Eine „kleinkarierte“ Tapete schmückt den Eingang zur Bergwohnung.***

Kilim rugs, fur bedspreads and much use of the colour red dominate in this little mountain home. ***Kelimteppiche, Felldecken und viel rote Farbe dominieren in dieser kleinen Bergwohnung.***

Monika Apponyi furnished this versatile attic room in Moroccan style.
Im marokkanischen Stil richtete Monika Apponyi dieses vielseitig nutzbare Zimmer unter dem Dach ein.

Fürstliche Bescheidenheit

Dies ist wahrscheinlich der bekannteste und meist fotografierte Getreidespeicher im ländlichen Gebiet von Salzburg. Ganz gewiss aber ist er der begehrteste. Denn nur auserwählten und engen Freundinnen und Freunden überlässt Salzburgs Grande Dame Fürstin Manni zu Sayn-Wittgenstein diesen blumengeschmückten alten Holzspeicher als Gästehäuschen. „Den Speicher haben wir Ende der sechziger Jahre in der Nähe von Weizenkirchen bei einem Bauern gekauft", erzählt Fürstin Manni und zeigt auf die Jahreszahl 1734, die in einen Balken im „Troatkasten" im Innern der Scheune geschnitzt ist, „und hier über die Hühnerleiter auf der Außenseite wurden damals die schweren Säcke voller Hafer, Gerste und Roggen nach oben geschleppt." Das verträumte Elmautal wurde 1956 das Zuhause der Fürstin. In diesem Jahr hat sie zusammen mit ihrem Ehemann Fürst Ludwig zu Sayn-Wittgenstein-Sayn begonnen, ihr Haupthaus zu bauen. „Wir haben es eigenhändig errichtet, mein Mann hat jeden Ziegel sieben mal in den Händen gehabt", erinnert sich die Fotografin und Ur-Ur-Ur-Ur-Enkelin von Kaiserin Maria Theresia, „dieses Jagdhaus, das Ernst von Demar gezeichnet hat, wurde unser neues Heim, nachdem das Familienschloss in Deutschland fünf Minuten vor Kriegsende durch Bomben gänzlich zerstört worden war." Heute verbringt die Fürstin, die als „Mamarazza" mit ihrem Fotoband voller Familien- und Gesellschaftsbilder bis nach New York gefeiert wurde, ihre Sommermonate im Elmautal zwischen ihrem Jagdhaus und dem schmucken Gästehäuschen. Und während der Festspielzeit ist die zwanzigfache Großmutter und sechsfache Urgroßmutter nicht nur ein gern gesehener Gast bei allen Konzerten, Opern, Empfängen, Diners und Cocktailparties, sondern gilt selbst als die Salzburger Gastgeberin schlechthin. Ihre sonntäglichen liebevoll zubereiteten Mittagessen – für achtzig bis hundert Gäste – gehören zu den gefragtesten Einladungen der Saison. Denn wer in der Welt der Musik, des Theaters, der Politik, der Aristokratie, der Wirtschaft, der Mode – oder einfach in ihrer eigenen Familie – zu Hause ist, der darf auf „Mannis" langer überdachter Terrasse und auf der Wiese vor dem Gästehäuschen an prachtvollen, in traditionellem grün und pink geschmückten Tafeln schlemmen und lachen und diskutieren und fabulieren und wenn es ihn gelüstet, eine Arie zum besten geben ...

Oben: Das Gästehäuschen von Fürstin Manni zu Sayn-Wittgenstein in der Nähe von Fuschl stammt aus dem Jahr 1734. Top: The little guesthouse near Fuschl run by Princess Manni zu Sayn-Wittgenstein dates back to 1734.

Rechts: Das alte prachtvolle Gästebett erwarb die Fürstin von einem fahrenden Bauern. Right: This splendid old guest's bed was acquired by the Princess from a travelling farmer.

Noble modesty

This is probably the best-known and most often photographed grain storehouse in the province of Salzburg. But without any doubt it is the most desirable. For the grande dame of Salzburg, Princess Manni zu Sayn-Wittgenstein, allows only a selection of her closest friends to use this old wooden storehouse, with its flowery decoration, as a guesthouse. "We bought it from a farmer near Weizenkirchen at the end of the 1960s," explains Princess Manni, pointing to the date 1734 carved on a beam inside the barn, "and here, on the outside, the chicken-ladder was formerly used to drag the heavy sacks of oats, barley and rye to the upper level." The sleepy Elmau valley became home to Princess Manni in 1956. In that year, she and her husband Prince Ludwig zu Sayn-Wittgenstein-Sayn began to build their main house. "We built it with our own hands; my husband handled each brick seven times," recalls the Princess, who is a photographer and the great-great-great-great-granddaughter of Empress Maria Theresia. "This hunting lodge, designed by Ernst von Demar, became our new home after the family mansion in Germany was totally destroyed by bombs, five minutes before the end of the war." Today the Princess, who has been celebrated as far as New York as "Mamarazza" for her photograph album full of family and society pictures, spends the summer months in the Elmau valley, between her hunting lodge and the pretty guesthouse.

During the annual Salzburg Festival, the grandmother of twenty and great-grandmother of six is not only a welcome guest at all concerts, operas, receptions, dinners and cocktail parties, but is herself considered the quintessential Salzburg hostess. Her lovingly prepared Sunday lunches – for eighty to a hundred guests – are among the most desirable events of the season. For anyone who is at home in the world of music, theatre, politics, aristocracy, industry or fashion – or simply in her own family – may be seen on Manni's long, roofed terrace or in the meadow in front of the guesthouse, at the splendid tables decked in the traditional green and pink, eating, laughing, arguing, telling stories, and perhaps even entertaining fellow guests with an aria …

Links: Die winzige Stube im Gästehaus zieren ein Porträt der Hausherrin, ein Teil einer Mostpresse von 1830 und ein Sofa mit antiker Paisleydecke. *Left: The tiny living room in the guesthouse is adorned with a portrait of the mistress of the house, part of a cider-press of 1830 and a sofa with an antique paisley cover.*

Oben: Blick vom Schlafzimmer auf den kleinen Balkon im ehemaligen Getreidespeicher. *Top: View from the bedroom of the little balcony in the former grain silo.*

Eine lauschige Jausenecke unter dem Dach auf dem schmalen Holzbalkon. *A snug little corner for afternoon snacks under the roof on the narrow wooden balcony.*

Alpine glamour with "edelweiss"

An enchanted spot where the foxes and hares say goodnight to each other ... Deer graze peacefully on the forecourt and sometimes venture a glance through the brightly lit windows. Yes, there really is such an idyll, in the Grisons mountains, in a little wood that surrounds a small three-hundred-year-old mountain farmhouse. Only a forest path, narrow but passable, leads to the pretty little sprucewood house. But there was a snag to the idyll. There were animals in the garden, but not enough room to live in comfort in the wooden house in the midst of the woods, even if only at weekends or during holiday periods. There was only a tiny kitchen, and no bathrooms at all. But Ruedi Haene from Zurich, the former owner of the Chesa Casanna, was a man of exceptional taste, of talent and, above all, of vision. So he immediately recognized how much potential lay hidden in his new "wretched" little house, and in order to create more room he first broke up the foundations and then had them excavated. In this way he acquired an extra floor, and with it, adequate living area for bedrooms, guestrooms and several bathrooms, a spacious kitchen-cum-dining room, a storage space for skis, and even a fitness room. Finally, he had everything covered with wood panelling so as to preserve the style of the house. But in the interior of his new realm, Ruedi Haene was able to indulge his tendency towards *Edelkitsch*. On the half-landings he built tiny, mirrored bathrooms, whose additional windows brought more light into the house. In the salon and dining room he boldly combined gold mirrors and crystal chandeliers from the time of Napoleon III with white-painted stags' antlers; he teamed cuckoo clocks with baroque candelabras. Whether it was a junk-shop find, a highly valued antique or a homemade accessory, Ruedi Haene, as he himself confessed at the time, could "really have his fling" in his Chesa Casanna (named after the mountain opposite). And he even had a name ready for his wittily audacious *Gesamtkunstwerk*: "Alpine glamour".

Alpen-Glamour mit Edelweiß

Ein verwunschener Ort, wo sich Füchse und Hasen gute Nacht sagen ... Rehe auf dem Vorplatz friedlich grasen und manchmal einen Blick durch die hell erleuchteten Fenster wagen. Nun, diese Idylle gibt es wirklich, und zwar in den Bündner Bergen, in einem Wäldchen, das ein kleines dreihundert Jahre altes Bergbauernhaus umgibt. Nur ein schmaler, allerdings befahrbarer Waldweg führt zu dem schmucken Häuschen aus Fichtenholz. Doch die Idylle hatte einen Haken: Es gab zwar Tiere im Garten, aber im Holzhaus mitten im Wald nicht genügend Platz, um darin – wenn auch nur am Wochenende oder in den Ferien – behaglich zu wohnen. Es existierte auch nur eine winzige Küche, und die Badezimmer fehlten gänzlich. Aber Ruedi Haene, der einstige Besitzer der Chesa Casanna, war ein Mann mit außerordentlichem Geschmack, mit Talent und vor allem mit Visionen. So erkannte der Zürcher sogleich, welch Potential in seinem neuen „armseligen" Häuschen versteckt war, und er ließ, um mehr Raum zu schaffen, als erstes das Fundament sprengen und danach ausbaggern. Auf diese Weise gewann er ein zusätzliches Stockwerk und damit genügend Wohnfläche für Schlaf-, Gäste- und mehrere Badezimmer, eine geräumige Wohnküche, eine Skiabstellkammer und sogar einen Fitnessraum. Zum Schluss wurde alles wieder mit Holz verkleidet, damit der Stil des Hauses bewahrt blieb. Im Innern seines neuen Reichs aber hat Ruedi Haene damals seinem Hang zum Edelkitsch freien Lauf lassen können. In den Treppenabsätzen baute er winzige verspiegelte Bäder ein, wobei zusätzliche Fenster mehr Licht ins Haus brachten. Goldspiegel und Kristalllüster aus der Zeit von Napoleon III kombinierte er im Salon und Esszimmer mutig mit weißgetünchten Hirschgeweihen; Kuckucksuhren paarte er mit Barockleuchtern. Ob Trödelfund, hoch gepriesene Antiquität oder selbst gebasteltes Accessoire, Ruedi Haene konnte sich, wie er damals selbst gestand, in seiner Chesa Casanna (benannt nach dem gegenüberliegenden Berg) „so richtig austoben". Und für sein witzig freches Gesamtkunstwerk hatte er sogar einen Namen parat: „Alpen-Glamour".

Top: The impressive roofed terrace next to the dining room annexe at the side of the Grisons chalet. ***Oben: Die eindrucksvolle überdachte Terrasse neben dem Esszimmeranbau auf der Seite des Bündner Chalets.***

Bottom left: "Snow flurry": a wooden room, all in white. ***Unten links: „Schneegestöber": eine Holzstube ganz in weiß.***

Bottom right: A successful mixture: modern art and dark wood. ***Unten rechts: Eine gelungene Mischung: moderne Kunst und dunkles Holz.***

A perfect solution: the owner built the missing bathrooms in mirrored corners. ***Perfekt gelöst: Die fehlenden Badezimmer baute der Hausherr in verspiegelte Ecken.***

Hospitality: a lovingly arranged reading corner in the bedroom. ***Gastfreundlich: liebevoll arrangierte Leseecke im Schlafzimmer.***

Long live kitsch! The master of the house was fond of striking arrangements. **Es lebe der Kitsch: Der Herr des Hauses liebte auffallende Arrangements.**

Mirrored in gold: the small dining room with an old crystal chandelier. **Golden gespiegelt: das kleine Esszimmer mit altem Kristallleuchter.**

Guest's four-poster bed: small but very romantic. **Gästebett mit Baldachin: klein, aber sehr romantisch.**

Wiesengeflüster

Ein sanfter Hügel folgt auf den nächsten. Die Felder und Wiesen leuchten in sattestem Grün. Vereinzelt trifft man hier auf ein von Blumenrabatten eingeschlossenes Gehöft. Immer weiter windet sich die Feldstraße im österreichischen Attergau durch die malerische Hügellandschaft. Die nächste Kuppe ist der Kronberg. Und da liegt es, das „Narzbergergut", das im Jahr 1250 zum erstenmal in einer Urkunde erwähnt wird. Es ist ein traditionelles Bauernhaus. „Wissenschaftlich gesehen ist es ein Rauchstubenhaus", präzisiert der Hausherr Professor Wolfgang Schuster und zeigt auf das dunkle Gebälk in der niedrigen Wohnstube. „Rauchstubenhaus heißt es, da in der Stube früher ein offenes Feuer gebrannt hat." Professor Schuster, Mitglied der Wiener Philharmoniker und Leiter des Pressereferats, kennt sich aus in der Geschichte des alten Hauses, das er vor etwa 25 Jahren – „es war damals ein Abbruchobjekt" – erworben hat. Mit unendlicher Sorgfalt hat der Musiker gemeinsam mit seiner Frau Christa das Bauernhaus sanft renoviert und ausgebaut. „Prominentester Besitzer des Hauses war Wolfgang Narz vom Kronberg", erzählt der Wiener, „er war ein ziemlich radikaler Bauernführer des Ersten Bauernaufstandes von 1525. Auf einem Balken des Daches ist er als kleines Männchen mit Fahne abgebildet." Das Innere des Bauernhauses – insgesamt zehn Zimmer mit Nebenräumen – hat das Ehepaar Schuster mit alten Möbeln aus der unmittelbaren Umgebung bestückt. Christa Schuster, Restauratorin an der Österreichischen

Das „Narzbergergut“ ist ein altes Rauchstubenhaus, das 1250 erstmals urkundlich erwähnt wurde.
The "Narzbergergut" is an old smokehouse first mentioned in documents of 1250.

Nationalbibliothek, hat nicht nur alle alten Stücke liebevoll restauriert, sondern auch in jahrelanger Millimeterarbeit die wunderbarsten Stickmuster auf unzählige Kissen, Tischdecken und Servietten gezaubert. Diese minutiös dekorierten Schätze schmücken nun die lange Eckbank in der Stube. Diese wiederum birgt noch zwei weitere Sammlungen. Zum einen ist es eine große Anzahl Silbergefäße aus der Zeit um 1900, zum anderen eine hübsche Kollektion ungewöhnlicher Heiligenbilder. “In Bauernhäusern war es früher Brauch, kleine Bilder von Namenspatronen der Bewohner aufzuhängen“, erläutert Professor Schuster, „wir haben dies noch etwas ausgeweitet, da meine Frau seit Jahren Votivbilder sammelt, wobei sich die kostbarsten Stücke in Wien befinden.“ Neben den alten umgebauten Räumen mit ihrem ländlichen Mobiliar und den vielen hübschen Objekten ist das „Narzbergergut“ auf dem Kronberg aber vor allem bekannt für einen neuen großen Saal – den von Professor Johannes Spalt entworfenen Konzertsaal in der ehemaligen Scheune. Hier finden während der Sommerwochen im Rahmen des beliebten „Attergauer Kultursommers“ zahlreiche Veranstaltungen statt. Und so kann sich Professor Wolfgang Schuster in dieser Zeit über einen wahrlich kurzen und bequemen Arbeitsweg freuen. Ist der Musiker doch auch der Künstlerische Leiter des „Attergauer Kultursommers“ und des Internationalen Orchesterinstituts Attergau für Wiener Klangstil unter der Schirmherrschaft der Wiener Philharmoniker.

Mit Passion von Christa Schuster gestickt und gesammelt: Tischleinen, Kissen und die antiken Heiligenbilder im „Herrgottswinkel" in der Stube. *Embroidered and collected with passion by Christa Schuster: table linen, cushions and the antique pictures of saints in "God's corner" in the living room.*

Whispering meadow

One gentle hill is followed by another. The fields and meadows shine in lushest green. We come across an isolated farmstead, enclosed by borders of flowers. The meadow path winds ever onward through the picturesque hill landscape in the Austrian Attergau district. The next hilltop is the Kronberg. And there it lies, the "Narzbergergut", first mentioned in a document of the year 1250. It is a traditional farmhouse. "From a scientific point of view, it is a smokehouse," the owner, Professor Wolfgang Schuster, specifies, indicating the dark wooden beams in the low-ceilinged living room. "It is given this name because an open fire used to burn in the room." Professor Schuster, a member of the Vienna Philharmonic Orchestra and director of its press office, is familiar with the history of the old house, which he bought some twenty-five years ago – "it was scheduled for demolition at the time". With endless care, the Viennese musician, together with his wife Christa, sensitively renovated and extended the farmhouse. "The most prominent owner of the house was Wolfgang Narz vom Kronberg," he explains. "He was quite a radical peasant leader during the First Peasant Rebellion of 1525. On one of the roof beams, a little man with a flag is depicted." The interior of the farmhouse – ten rooms altogether, with some side rooms – has been furnished by the Schusters with old pieces of furniture from the nearby area. Christa Schuster, a restorer at the Austrian National Library, has not only lovingly restored all the old furniture, but has also painstakingly conjured up over many years the most wonderful embroidery patterns on countless cushions, tablecloths and napkins. These meticulously decorated treasures now adorn the long corner bench in the living room. This room in turn houses two further collections. One consists of a large number of peasant silver containers from the late nineteenth to early twentieth century, and the other is a charming collection of unusual portrayals of saints. "It used to be the custom in farmhouses to hang up small pictures of the owners' patron saints," recounts Professor Schuster, "and we have extended the idea somewhat, since my wife has been collecting votive pictures for years, although the most valuable examples are in Vienna." Apart from the old rebuilt rooms with their country furnishings and the many attractive objects, the "Narzbergergut" on the Kronberg is best known for a new, large hall – the concert hall designed by Professor Johannes Spalt in the former barn. Here many events are held during the summer weeks as part of the popular Attergau Summer of Culture. This means that, during that period, Professor Wolfgang Schuster has the advantage of a truly short and convenient "journey" to work. After all, this musician is also the artistic director of the Attergau Summer of Culture and of the Attergau International Orchestral Institute for Viennese Musical Style, under the patronage of the Vienna Philharmonic Orchestra.

Diese Bauernstube wie aus dem Märchenbuch gehört zum „Narzbergergut" in Oberösterreich.
This peasant living-room, like something out of a fairy-tale, is part of the "Narzbergergut" in Upper Austria.

Eine weitere Schuster-Kollektion: altes Bauernsilber in einer Holzvitrine. *Another Schuster collection: old peasant silver in a wooden display case.*

A riot of colour Farbenfreude

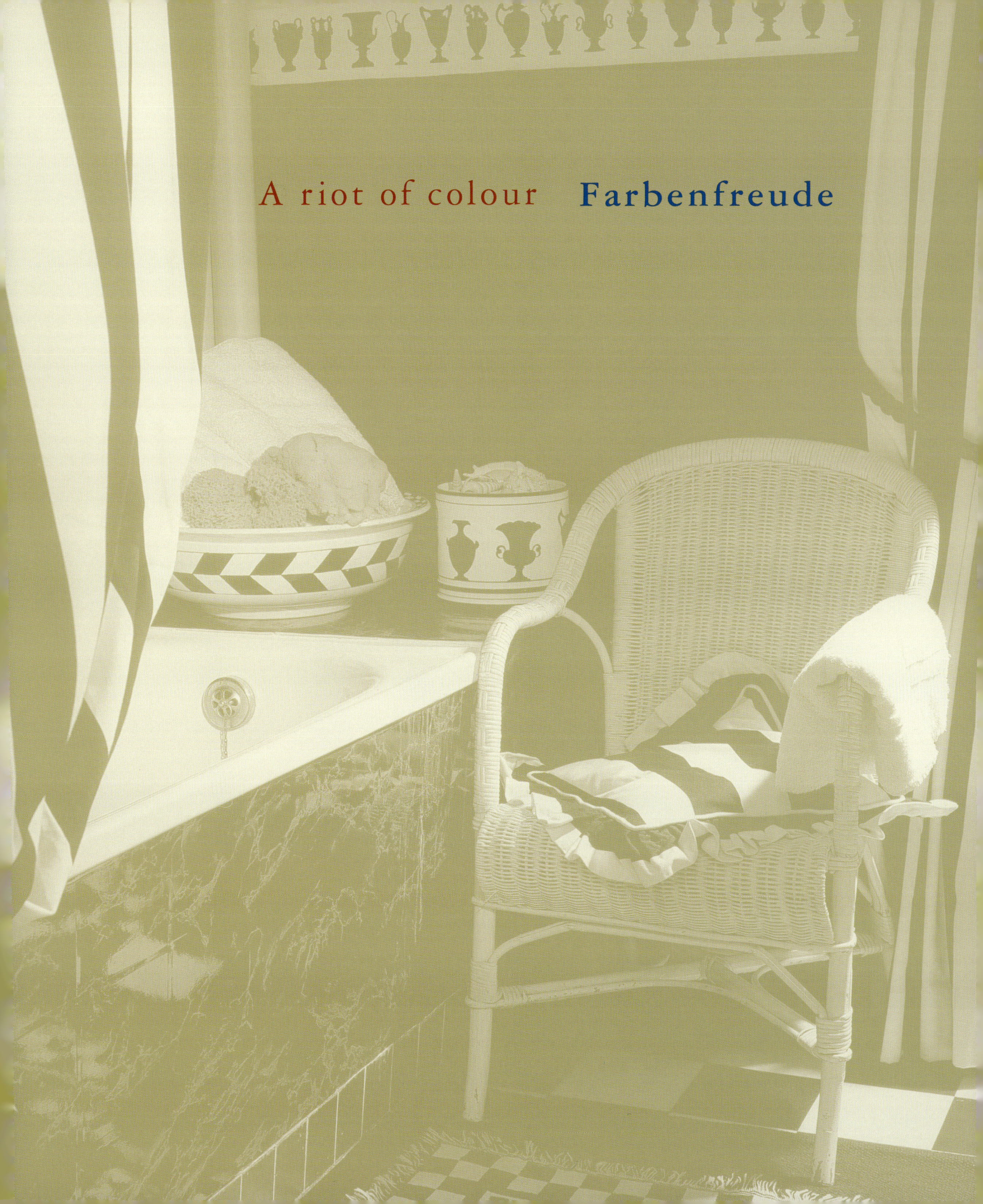

Top left: Well-being among the ice: afternoon snacks on the terrace of the Bogner house. ***Oben links: Eisiges Wohlbefinden: Jause auf der Terrasse des Bogner-Hauses.***

Top right: Well guarded: the entrance to the "Chesetta da l'Urs" near St Moritz. ***Oben rechts: Gut bewacht ist der Eingang in die „Chesetta da l'Urs" bei St. Moritz.***

Winter atmosphere "à l'americaine" in the house of Willy and Sônia Bogner. ***Winterliche Stimmung „à l'americaine" im Haus von Willy und Sônia Bogner.***

Bear's burrow

He loves the world of American Indians with their exciting tribal cultures, he loves the simple prairie life of the cowboys. And above all he loves mountains, snow and ice. The steeper and more dangerous, the better. And it is this love of wild, unadulterated nature that Willy Bogner has also brought to the Swiss Engadine, to a little secluded wood away from the society bustle of St Moritz, a quiet, exclusive neighbourhood. Here is a simple log cabin where the fashion designer and director of films on winter sports retreats for a few weeks every winter, with his wife Sônia and their two children Florinda and Bernhard. The chalet was built in 1964 by Willy Bogner's mother, Maria Bogner, the woman who invented stretch ski-pants, that practical garment for winter sports; the woman who in 1948, together with Willy Bogner senior, laid the foundation stone for the international Bogner fashion empire. Their mountain home was to be simple, of moderate size, and unpretentious, but built high enough to allow room for Bogner senior's finest trophy – a gigantic, splendid Kodiak bear. It was this bear that gave the wooden house its name: "Chesetta da l'Urs". And indeed, above and below the mighty Alaskan bear that hangs on the wooden wall above the corner dining area, there are just two centimetres of dark beams to be seen. "That's what I call made to measure," laughs Willy Bogner, who has just returned from a strenuous day of filming skiing, and is making himself comfortable in "his" corner of the long sofa. Twice an Olympic competitor and a multiple German ski champion, this afternoon Bogner has once again donned his skis, armed himself with his film camera, and whizzed down the St Moritz bobsleigh run – "at about 90 kilometres per hour". One of Willy Bogner's favourite pieces in the "Chesetta da l'Urs" is a colourful, large-format picture hanging as a central focus of attention in the living room. The portrait is by the Native American artist Nieto. "The most important thing in the picture is the bow," the top sportsman and fashion designer explains to visitors, "because the name Bogner – bowman – comes from 'bow-making'." The big Indian painting is only one of many objects in the "bear's burrow" in the middle of the Swiss mountains that remind one of Santa Fe, New Mexico. Some of the tasselled and feathered lamps in the Bogner retreat, for example, were made by Indians. And the fireplace is adorned by a black cowboy relief in wrought iron, also originating from the American West. "But the US look is not intentional," says Bogner. "This is just the result of countless holidays at our house in Colorado, where we like to ride all day through the wild terrain. And anyway," he adds quickly, "we design fashion, not our holiday homes." In winter, of course, they go skiing, and Willy Bogner comments laughingly that his South American wife Sônia uses "the Brazilian style of skiing". Snowboarding incidentally is just as much part of the repertoire as glacier climbing. "The most important thing," Bogner stresses, "is being in the open air," and luckily the Engadine mountains still have many undiscovered peaks, slopes, caves and valleys …

Bärenhaus

Er liebt die Welt der Indianer mit ihren spannenden Stammeskulturen, er liebt das einfache Prärieleben der amerikanischen Cowboys. Und er liebt vor allem Berge, Schnee und Eis. Je steiler und gefährlicher desto besser. Und diese Liebe zur wilden unverfälschten Natur hat Willy Bogner auch ins schweizerische Engadin gebracht: in ein kleines Wäldchen abseits vom Society-Rummel von St. Moritz mit ruhiger exklusiver Nachbarschaft. Hierher, in ein einfaches Blockhaus, zieht sich der Modemacher und Wintersportfilmer mit seiner Frau Sônia und den beiden Kindern Florinda und Bernhard jeweils für ein paar Wochen im Winter zurück. Gebaut hat das Chalet im Jahr 1964 die Mutter Willy Bogners: Maria Bogner, jene Frau, die die Stretchkeilhose, dieses für den Wintersport so praktische Kleidungsstück, erfunden hat. Die Frau, die zusammen mit Willy Bogner Senior 1948 den Grundstein für das internationale Bogner-Modeimperium gelegt hatte. Einfach sollte ihr Berghaus sein, nicht groß, und ohne Chichi, aber doch so hoch, dass genug Platz vorhanden ist für Vater Bogners schönste Trophäe – einen riesengroßen prächtigen Kodiak-Bären. Der hat übrigens dem Holzhaus auch den Namen gegeben: „Chesetta da l'Urs". Und wirklich, oben und unterhalb des gewaltigen Alaska-Bärs, der auf der Holzwand über der Essecke hängt, gibt es noch genau zwei Zentimeter dunkle Balken zu sehen. „So etwas nennt man Maßarbeit", lacht Willy Bogner, der gerade von einem anstrengenden Skifilmtag heimkommt und es sich in „seinem" Eck auf dem langen Sofa gemütlich macht. Der zweifache Olympiateilnehmer und mehrfache deutsche Meister ist an diesem Nachmittag einmal mehr auf Skiern und mit der Filmkamera bewaffnet den Eiskanal der St. Moritzer Bobbahn hinuntergezischt – „mit ungefähr 90 Stundenkilometern". Zu Willy Bogners Lieblingsstücken in der „Chesetta da l'Urs" zählt ein farbiges, großformatiges Bild, das als zentraler Blickpunkt im Wohnzimmer hängt. Das Porträt stammt vom indianischen Künstler Nieto. „Das Wichtigste auf dem Bild ist der Bogen", erklärt der Topsportler und Modemann jedem Besucher, „denn der Name ‚Bogner' leitet sich ab von ‚Bogenmachen'." Das große Indianerbild ist nur eines von vielen Objekten, die im „Bärenhaus" mitten in den Schweizer Bergen an Santa Fe im US-Staat New Mexico erinnern. So wurden auch einige der geschnürten und gefederten Lampen im Bogner-Refugium von Indianern hergestellt. Und den Kamin schmückt ein schwarzes Cowboy-Relief aus Schmiedeeisen, das ebenfalls aus dem amerikanischen Westen stammt. „Der US-Look ist aber nicht etwa gewollt", so der Hausherr, „dies ist nur das Resultat unzähliger Ferienaufenthalte in unserem Haus in Colorado, wo wir am liebsten tagelang durchs wilde Gelände reiten. Und überhaupt", fügt er noch schnell hinzu, „designen tun wir unsere Mode und nicht unsere Ferienhäuser." Im Winter wird selbstverständlich Ski gefahren, wobei Willy Bogner lachend meint, seine südamerikanische Frau Sônia fahre schon eher „den brasilianischen Skistil". Unterwegs sein mit dem Snowboard gehört übrigens für den Unternehmer genauso zum Repertoire wie Gletscherklettern. „Das Allerwichtigste ist die Bewegung in der freien Natur", betont Bogner, und in den Engadiner Bergen gäbe es zum Glück noch viele unentdeckte Gipfel, Hänge, Höhlen und Täler ...

Long live the Wild West: the metal cowboys come from Arizona. **Es lebe der Wilde Westen: Die Metall-Cowboys stammen aus Arizona.**

Made to measure: the Alaskan bear fits precisely on the wall of the log cabin. ***Maßarbeit: Der Alaska-Bär passt haargenau auf die Blockhüttenwand.***

Indian tradition in the bear's burrow: the portrait is by the Native American artist Nieto. ***Indianisches im Bärenhaus: Das Porträt entwarf der von den Indianern abstammende Maler Nieto.***

Memories of Santa Fe in the Engadine mountains. ***Reminiszenz an Santa Fe in den Engadiner Bergen.***

Sammelwut

Wo der Lehrer in diesem ehemaligen Klassenzimmer sein Pult platziert hatte, wissen wir nicht genau. Dass seine Schüler aber sehnsuchtsvoll durch die großen Fenster hinaus in die paradiesische Berglandschaft geschaut haben, ist überlieferte Tatsache. Und dass sowohl Lehrer wie Schüler am liebsten im heutigen umgebauten Wohnzimmer Unterricht gehabt hätten, steht außer Frage. Denn das über hundert Quadratmeter große ebenerdige Zimmer im Klosterser Chalet „Montana“ ist wohl das ungewöhnlichste „Schulzimmer“ der Schweiz. 1952 wurde das vierstöckige Holzhaus gebaut und als alpine Bildungsstätte genutzt. Dann diente es als Hotel-Dependance (unter anderem für den amerikanischen Schriftsteller Irvin Shaw) und wurde schließlich in zwei Wohnungen unterteilt. Neben vielen Holztönen sind Grün und Rot die dominierenden Farben im lang gezogenen „Montana“-Wohnraum, der mit Hilfe verschiedener Sitzgruppen und einer Essecke unterteilt ist. „Damit herrscht bei uns das ganze Jahr Weihnachtsstimmung“, gibt die Hausfrau und Mutter dreier Jugendlicher zu, „doch diese Farbkombination ist stimmungsvoll und kreiert die perfekte Atmosphäre, die wir in den Bergen suchen.“ Unterstrichen wird das urige Ambiente durch eine Vielzahl von Holzgegenständen, deren Ursprung augenscheinlich ist: Bären aus dem Berner Oberland. „Wo immer ich hingehe, zu Auktionen, auf Flohmärkte oder in kleine Antiquitätengeschäfte, überall halte ich Ausschau nach Holzbären“, gesteht die charmante Hausfrau, „ob es einzelne Bären sind oder Bärenbilderrahmen, Bärenaschenbecher, Bärenlampenfüße, ob groß oder klein, alt oder neu, ich muss diese Dinger einfach haben.“ Die meisten der dekorativen Holzbären wurden Anfang des letzten Jahrhunderts geschnitzt und als Berner Souvenirs aus der Schweiz nach Hause gebracht. Einige Bären zieren auch den Steinkamin, den der bekannte Bündner Kunstmaler Alois Carigiet mit Szenen aus der Bergwelt bemalt hat. Die Schlafzimmer im oberen Stock sind einfach und unprätentiös gehalten. Genauso wie der Eingangsbereich mit dem leuchtend roten Teppichboden. Denn die Hauptrolle im Chalet „Montana“ spielen Walli und Gilly, die beiden Hunde der Familie – und natürlich die hölzernen Bären.

Gut bewacht: Labrador Gilli auf der langen Terrasse im Chalet „Montana“.

On guard: Gilli the labrador on the long terrace at the Chalet “Montana”.

Collecting mania

Where exactly the teacher's desk was positioned in this former classroom, we do not know. But that his pupils gazed longingly through the large windows to the magnificent mountain landscape outside is a recorded fact. And that both teacher and students would have much preferred to have their lessons in the present, rebuilt living room is unquestionable. For this ground-level room of more than a hundred square metres in the Klosters Chalet "Montana", is probably the most unusual "classroom" in Switzerland. This four-storey wooden house was built in 1952 and used as an Alpine cultural centre. Then it was used as a hotel extension (for the American writer Irwin Shaw, among others) and was finally divided into two apartments. Apart from many shades of wood, green and red are the dominant colours in the long Montana living room, which is subdivided with the help of several groups of seats and a dining corner. "We sort of have Christmas all the year round," admits the hostess and mother of three children, "but this combination of colours is very evocative and creates the perfect atmosphere that we look for in the mountains." The traditional environment is underlined by a number of wooden objects, whose origin is obvious: bears from the Bernese Oberland. "Wherever I go, to auctions, flea markets or small antique shops, I look out for wooden bears," confesses the charming housewife, "whether they are simply bears, or bear picture frames, bear ashtrays, bear lamp feet, whether big or small, old or new, I just have to have the things." Most of these decorative wooden bears were carved in the early twentieth century and brought home from Switzerland as souvenirs of Berne. Some of the bears also adorn the stone fireplace, painted by the well-known local artist Alois Carigiet with scenes from the mountain world. The bedrooms on the upper floor are kept simple and unpretentious, as is the entrance area with its brilliant red carpet. For the main role at the Chalet "Montana" is played by Walli and Gilly, the two family dogs – and of course the wooden bears.

Oben links: Der bekannte Bündner Maler Alois Carigiet dekorierte den Kamin im Chalet „Montana". *Top left: The well-known Grisons painter Alois Carigiet decorated the fireplace at the Chalet "Montana".*

Oben rechts: Hauptsache geschnitzt: eine kleine Auswahl der großen Holzsammlung, die die Hausherrin im Laufe der Jahre zusammengetragen hat. *Top right: As long as it's carved: a small selection of the large collection of wooden items that the mistress of the house has gathered over the years.*

Auch als Garderobenständer muss ein Holzbär herhalten.
A wooden bear is brought into service as a coat-stand.

Das Elternschlafzimmer mit eingebauten Holzbetten und rot karierter Bettwäsche. *The parent's bedroom with built-in wooden beds and red checked bedlinen.*

Die Essecke im ehemaligen Schulzimmer ist in rot und grün gehalten. *The dining corner in the former schoolroom is decorated in red and green.*

Wandspiele in Farbe Wall games in colour

Ein rotes Gästezimmer, ein helles, graublaues Kinderzimmer, ein flaschengrünes Schlafzimmer, ein dunkelblaues Entree, ein schwarz-weißes Bad und eine kanariengelbe Küche. In dieser Bergwohnung ist wahrlich keine Wand verschont geblieben – die Ausgangslage rief nach kreativen Ideen. Anstelle des gewünschten alten Holzhäuschens wurde es schließlich eine Stadtwohnung aus der Zeit um 1900, die zum neuen Winterdomizil einer vierköpfigen Familie mit zwei Hunden werden sollte. Die Räume waren zwar nicht groß, dafür aber hoch, das Wohnzimmer mit Holz verkleidet und der Balkon samt Fernsicht absolut perfekt. Um nun in diesen fünf Zimmern ein gemütliches Winterambiente zu kreieren, beschlossen die neuen Wohnungsinhaber in die Farbtöpfe beziehungsweise in die Tapetenrollen zu steigen. Warme Farbtöne waren angesagt, die sich mit den verschiedenen alten Holzmöbeln und den diversen Sammlungen der Hausfrau vertragen mussten. Das Resultat ist ein farbiges Kaleidoskop: dunkle Eiche auf rauchblauer Streifenwand, helle Tanne auf himbeerroter toile de Jouy-Tapete, großblumiges Leinen im Holzsalon, schwarzer Klebetapeten-„Marmor" fürs Bad und leuchtend gelbe Farbe als perfekter Hintergrund für eine Sammlung antiker, blau-weißer Speiseplatten aus England in der kleinen Wohnküche. Dieser charmante Allzweckraum – er ist Spielzimmer, Arbeitsecke, Diskussionsstube und Esszimmer zugleich – verdient die ihm von zahlreichen Freunden verliehene Bezeichnung der „Gummizelle". Denn das knapp zwölf Quadratmeter große gelbe Speisezimmer mit dem drei Quadratmeter großen Küchenanbau kann bis zu sechzehn Gäste beherbergen – sogar sitzend!

A guestroom in red, a nursery in pale blue-grey, a bedroom in bottle green, an entrance hall in dark blue, a bathroom in black and white, and a kitchen in canary yellow. In this mountain home, not one wall has been spared – the initial situation called for creative ideas. The little old wooden house that had been the original objective was finally transformed into a fin-de-siècle town apartment, which was to become the new winter residence of a family of four with two dogs. The rooms were not big but they were high-ceilinged, the living room was wood-panelled, and the balcony with a view was absolutely perfect. To create a cosily winter atmosphere in these five rooms, the new inhabitants decided, as it were, to dip into pots of paint and climb into rolls of wallpaper. Warm tones were called for, which had to harmonize with the various items of old wooden furniture and the diverse collections of the mistress of the house. The result was a colourful kaleidoscope: dark oak with a wall striped in smoky blue, light pine with raspberry red toile de Jouy wallpaper, linen with a large floral pattern in the wooden salon, black adhesive "marble" wallpaper for the bathroom and brilliant yellow as a perfect background for a collection of antique blue and white dinner plates from England in the small kitchen-diner. This charming all-purpose room – it is a playroom, work corner, discussion parlour and dining room at the same time – deserves the nickname of "padded cell" bestowed on it by countless guests. For this yellow dining room of barely twelve square metres with the kitchen annexe of three square metres can hold up to sixteen guests – even sitting down!

Einst ein Ofen, heute als Dessert-büfett gebraucht. *Once a stove, today used as a sideboard for desserts.*

***Vollgepfropft:* Im blauen Gang steht ein antiker englischer „oak dresser", gegenüber an der Wand hängen alte Ornamentstiche aus Prag.** *Crammed full: an English oak dresser stands in the blue corridor, and on the wall opposite hang old ornamental prints from Prague.*

In der Wohnküche hängen blauweiße alte Platten auf leuchtend gelben Mauern. *In the kitchen-cum-diner, old blue and white plates hang on gleaming yellow walls.*

Selbst gebastelt: Der schwarze „Marmor" im Badezimmer stammt von der Rolle. *Do it yourself: the black "marble" in the bathroom comes off a roll.*

Rechts: Blick in die Drei-Quadratmeter-Küche. Der „Tellerrand" um die Tür ist eine Tapete. *Right: A view of the three-square-metre kitchen. The "edging" around the door is wallpaper.*

Fridolin Spörri
Achermüller in
Eschenbach

Made to measure **Maßarbeit**

A decorative concept? No, we never had anything like that! As far as we are concerned, a house must be labrador-friendly, ski-boot-compatible, and as low-maintenance as possible," say the occupants of the Chalet "Sweenix" on the Russna in Klosters, in the Grisons. Anyone who visits the spacious house designed by the Davos architect Norbert Friedel and completed in 1987 after only six months of construction not only reaches the highest-placed house on the sunniest hill of the well-known winter sports resort, but at the same time is transported into a quite individual world. The interior is a daring mixture. Many of the decorative objects and collectors' items that hang, stand or lie distributed throughout the house were once stored in the loft of the female owner's parental home in Ohio, USA. "Here, for instance, are my mother's riding boots and my father's collection of old tools, and an Amazon paddle that I brought from America, just as I did the old fishing rods and the skiing and winter sports posters. The wooden skis on the wall in the dining room, on the other hand, belonged to my husband's grandfather. He used them only once – for his regiment's military exercise on a visit by Emperor Wilhelm just before World War I. But the whole demonstration was actually a complete bluff, since only a very few members of the troop knew how to ski ..." The American and Swiss finds were framed in a living area of high walls, outsize windows, a natural stone floor and an impressive structure of beams directly under the roof. The centrepiece of this spacious and yet intimate area is the fireplace, open on two sides. Its frame, too – like so much at the Chalet "Sweenix" – is "extra large", made of sizable silver-grey-green rock fragments from the nearby Flüelapass, and the owner of the house himself approved every piece of rock ...

Ein Dekorationskonzept? Nein, so etwas hatten wir nie! Bei uns muss ein Haus Labrador-gefällig, Skischuh-freundlich und möglichst pflegeleicht sein," heißt es im Chalet „Sweenix" auf der Russna im bündnerischen Klosters. Wer dem weitläufigen Haus, das der Davoser Architekt Norbert Friedel entworfen hat und das nach einer nur sechsmonatigen Konstruktionszeit im Jahr 1987 fertig wurde, einen Besuch abstattet, der fährt nicht nur hinauf zum höchstgelegenen Haus am sonnigsten Hügel des bekannten Wintersportortes, sondern wird gleichzeitig auch in eine ganz eigene Welt entführt. Eine mutige Mischung macht das Interieur aus. Viele der Dekorationsobjekte und Sammlerstücke, die im ganzen Haus verteilt hängen, stehen oder liegen, befanden sich nämlich einst auf dem Speicher des elterlichen Zuhauses der Besitzerin im amerikanischen Bundesstaat Ohio. „Da sind zum Beispiel die Reitstiefel meiner Mutter oder die Sammlung alter Werkzeuge meines Vaters, ein Amazonas-Paddel, das ich aus Amerika mitbrachte, genauso wie die alten Fischerutensilien oder die Ski- und Wintersportposters. Die Holzski an der Wand im Esszimmer hingegen gehörten dem Großvater meines Mannes. Der brauchte das Paar nur ein einziges Mal – für eine Militärübung seines Regiments beim Besuch Kaiser Wilhelms kurz vor dem Ersten Weltkrieg. Die ganze Demonstration war aber eigentlich ein großer Bluff, da nur ein ganz kleiner Teil der Truppe wusste, wie man Ski fährt…" Eingerahmt werden die amerikanisch-schweizerischen Trouvaillen im Wohnbereich von hohen Mauern, übergroßen Fenstern, einem Natursteinboden und einer eindrucksvollen Balkenkonstruktion direkt unter dem Dach. Das Kernstück dieses geräumigen und trotzdem intimen Raumes ist der nach zwei Seiten offene Kamin. Auch die Kaminumrandung ist – wie vieles im Chalet „Sweenix" – „extra large", aus großen silbergrau-grünen Felsbrocken vom benachbarten Flüelapass, wobei der Hausbesitzer jedes Stück Stein persönlich für gut befunden hat ...

Patient work proves effective: dried flowers above an old peasant bed. ***Geduldsarbeit mit großer Wirkung: getrocknete Blumen über einem alten Bauernbett.***

A house for guests: the salon with the Flüela stone fireplace is the venue for many interesting encounters. ***Ein Haus für Gäste: Der Salon mit dem Flüela-Steinkamin ist Ort vieler interessanter Begegnungen.***

A servant receives guests: a wooden figure next to an antique wooden chair in the entrance hall. **Hier empfängt der Diener: Holzfigur neben antikem Holzstuhl im Entree.**

"Ski-crowned": the dining table in the mountain house on the Russna. **„Ski-gekrönt": der Esstisch im Berghaus auf der Russna.**

The architecture of the Klosters chalet is slightly reminiscent of houses in Aspen in America. ***Ein bisschen erinnert die Ansicht des Chalets in Klosters an Häuser im amerikanischen Aspen.***

Under a high beamed ceiling: the bedroom with a view of the Gotschna peak. ***Unter hoher Balkendecke: das Schlafzimmer mit Blick auf die „Gotschna"-Spitze.***

A life of one's own Eigenleben

Summit in Davos

It measures 254 x 443 cm, is made of heavy iron and bears the title "L'albero" ("The Tree"). This mighty work by the contemporary Italian artist Enzo Cucchi is the centrepiece of the grand and spaciously laid out "Villa Seehof", above Davos. When the World Economic Forum is held annually in January in the mountain region of the Grisons, the Alpine domicile of Susi Stahel is transformed into an important meeting-place for a swarm of international guests, made up of heads of state, business people, bankers and diplomats. Enzo Cucchi's "Tree", which adorns the large wall of the salon where intensive discussions take place at almost all times of the day and night during the conference, has thus become a symbol of understanding and cooperation. "The peace talks between Hosni Mubarak, Benjamin Netanyahu and Yasser Arafat took place in this living room," the owner relates with a touch of pride, "and even the President of Uzbekistan stayed here during the Forum days for two years running." Today, murals in the entrance hall still recall the visit of this important guest from Central Asia, who on both occasions arrived at the Stahel residence with a delegation of thirty staff members. This splendid property on the hill above the city, which was intended as a family house for the Stahels, is sought out during these days of international economic discussion not only by illustrious guests but above all by an unusual number of visitors. "During this period we cater for between fifty and two hundred guests and run a twenty-four-hour business." That the "Villa Seehof" is so much in demand as a five-star private hotel is certainly due to its unique location, its many bedrooms and its curved indoor swimming pool. The interior, too, is worth a look. The Italian decorator Celeste d'Anna, a friend of the owner, has lent a quality of casual elegance to the light-filled rooms, with Italian hand-printed fabrics, silk taffeta from Rubelli and cashmere from Pierre Frey.

Top left: A very special bathroom. ***Oben links: Ein Badezimmer der ganz besonderen Art.***

Top right: The indoor swimming pool is designed in a gentle curve. ***Oben rechts: In einem leichten Bogen ist der Indoor-Swimmingpool angelegt.***

Right: Grand and yet countrified: the entrance to the Stahel property in the Grisons. ***Rechts: Herrschaftlich und doch ländlich: der Eingang ins Stahel-Anwesen im Bündnerland.***

Left: A blaze of colour: A French chair in front of a screen.
Links: Farbenpracht: französischer Sessel vor einem Paravent.

Right: A festive atmosphere in the "Villa Seehof".
Rechts: festliche Stimmung in der „Villa Seehof".

Gipfeltreffen in Davos

Es misst 254 mal 443 Zentimeter, ist aus schwerem Eisen und trägt den Titel „L'Albero" („Der Baum"). Das gewaltige Werk des italienischen Gegenwartskünstlers Enzo Cucchi ist das Herzstück der großzügig und weitläufig angelegten „Villa Seehof" oberhalb von Davos. Wenn in der graubündnerischen Bergwelt jeweils im Januar das bekannte „World Economic Forum" stattfindet, verwandelt sich das Bergdomizil von Susi Stahel in einen wichtigen Treffpunkt für eine internationale Gästeschar, die sich aus Staatsoberhäuptern, Businessleuten, Bankiers und auch Diplomaten zusammensetzt. Enzo Cucchis „Baum", der die große Wand des Salons schmückt, in dem während der Wirtschaftstagung fast zu jeder Tages- und Nachtzeit intensive Gespräche stattfinden, wird so zu einem Sinnbild für Verständigung und gemeinsames Wirken. „Die Friedensgespräche zwischen Hosni Mubarak, Benjamin Netanyahu und Yasser Arafat haben in diesem Wohnzimmer stattgefunden", erzählt die Hausherrin nicht ohne Stolz, „auch der Präsident von Usbekistan wohnte während der Forum-Tage zwei Jahre hintereinander bei uns." Noch heute erinnern Wandmalereien im Entree an den hohen Gast aus Zentralasien, der jeweils mit einer dreißig Mann starken Delegation in der Stahel-Residenz eintraf. Dieses herrliche Anwesen auf dem Hügel über der Stadt, das als Familienhaus für die Stahel-Familie konzipiert ist, suchen während dieser internationalen Wirtschaftstagung nicht nur illustre, sondern vor allem auch ungewöhnlich zahlreiche Besucher auf. „Wir bewirten hier oben während dieser Zeit zwischen fünfzig und zweihundert Gäste und sind ein vierundzwanzig-Stunden-Betrieb." Dass die „Villa Seehof" so gefragt ist als „Fünf-Sterne-Privathotel" liegt sicherlich an ihrer einzigartigen Lage, den vielen Schlafzimmern und an ihrem in einem Bogen angelegten Indoor-Swimmingpool. Auch das Interieur darf sich sehen lassen. Der Italiener Celeste dell'Anna, ein Freund der Hausherrin, hat den hellen Räumen mit italienischen handbedruckten Stoffen aus Italien, mit Seidentaft von „Rubelli" und Kaschmir von „Pierre Frey" Eleganz und Lässigkeit verliehen.

Right: An open stairwell indoors with rope handrails links the entrance hall to a workroom on the first floor. **Rechts: Ein offenes Treppenhaus im Innern mit Seilgeländer verbindet den Eingangsraum mit einem Arbeitsraum im ersten Stock.**

"L'albero", an artwork in iron by Enzo Cucchi, is the centrepiece of the mountain villa, furnished in contemporary style. **„L'albero", ein Kunstwerk aus Eisen, stammt von Enzo Cucchi und ist das Herzstück der modern eingerichteten Bergvilla.**

"Curvaceous": the cosy room with a fireplace next door to the salon. **„Kurvenreich": das behagliche Kaminzimmer direkt neben dem Salon.**

Natur pur   Simply nature

Drei Themen ist dieses Haus in Salieto im Südtirol gewidmet: der vergänglichen Schönheit der Natur, der einzigartigen Patina antiker Dinge und dem unverwechselbaren Wohlgeruch der norditalienischen Küche. Sie alle haben etwas mit Leidenschaft zu tun, mit „passione“ für das, was uns umgibt und uns bewegt. Der Besitzer dieses eindrucksvollen Hauses in der Nähe von Cortina d'Ampezzo, der Maler Renato Balsamo, personifiziert diese Leidenschaft. Seine Gemälde, die im Studio unter dem Dach – auf dem umgebauten ehemaligen Heuboden – entstehen, sind Zeichen eines neugierigen Geistes und einer tiefen Verehrung der Natur: ein einzelner Baum, ein Stillleben mit Früchten, ein Fels, der aus dem Meer ragt, eine Berglandschaft. Da sind aber auch seine Porträts. Renato Balsamo malt Gesichter mit der gleichen Sorgfalt und Präzision, mit der er sich der Natur nähert. Überall stehen die farbenprächtigen Bilder herum in diesem mit einem Oberlicht versehenen Dachatelier. Und sind die feinen Balsamo-Porträts nicht auf Leinwand gebannt, finden sie sich auf Tellern, Platten oder glatten, wohlgeformten Steinen aus dem Flussbett in der Nähe des Hauses. Denn vor diesem Maler ist kein Untergrund sicher. Das Landhaus von Renato und Mina Balsamo stammt aus dem achtzehnten Jahrhundert und ist angefüllt mit traditionellen antiken Möbeln und Objekten aus der Gegend. Schon am Eingang, den man über eine Holztreppe erreicht, wartet eine dreihundert Jahre alte Mühltrommel auf die Ankömmlinge. Im Innern des alten Hauses – in der Stube und dem Ofenzimmer –, da halten Barockfiguren Wache, und antike Haushaltsutensilien sowie bäuerliche Gebrauchsgegenstände werden zu dekorativen Zwecken eingesetzt. Und dann sind da noch die betörenden Düfte aus der Küche. Wie schon ihre berühmte Tante Donna Rachele, ist auch Mina Balsamo eine begnadete Köchin. Drum, wer hier zum Essen bleiben darf, der sollte die Einladung nicht ausschlagen ...

This house in Salieto, in South Tyrol, is dedicated to three themes: the transitory beauty of nature, the unique patina of antique objects and the unmistakable aroma of north Italian cuisine. They all have something to do with a passion for what surrounds us and what moves us. The owner of this impressive house near Cortina d'Ampezzo, the painter Renato Balsamo, personifies this passion. His paintings, which are created in the studio below the roof – in the converted hayloft – denote a spirit of curiosity and a deep veneration for nature: a single tree, a still life with fruit, a rock jutting out of the sea, a mountain landscape. Then there are his portraits. Renato Balsamo paints faces with the same care and precision with which he approaches nature. These colourful pictures are to be seen placed all around this roof-lit attic studio. And those of the superb Balsamo portraits that are not to be found on canvas appear on plates, dishes, or smooth, well-formed stones from the riverbed near the house. For no medium is safe from this painter. The country house owned by Renato and Mina Balsamo dates from the eighteenth century, and is filled with traditional antique furniture and objects from the local area. At the entrance, reached by means of a wooden staircase, a three-hundred-year-old mill-drum stands to greet new arrivals. Within the old house – in the living room and the room containing the stove – Baroque figures stand guard, and antique household utensils as well as peasant implements are placed for decorative effect. And then you have the bewitching aromas from the kitchen. Just like her famous aunt, Donna Rachele, Mina Balsamo is a highly gifted cook. So anyone who is allowed to stay for dinner here should accept the invitation with enthusiasm ...

Das Zuhause des Künstlers Renato Balsamo in Cortina d'Ampezzo: ein Bauernhaus aus dem achtzehnten Jahrhundert. *The home of the artist Renato Balsamo at Cortina d'Ampezzo: an eighteenth-century farmhouse.*

Auf dem ehemaligen Heuboden hat Renato Balsamo das Atelier untergebracht. Die Bilder erzählen von seiner Liebe zur Natur.
The former hayloft now accommodates Renato Balsamo's studio. The pictures are evidence of his love of nature.

Den Eingang des Hauses schmücken ein Getreidemühlrad, diverse Körbe und Brennholz für kalte Wintertage. *The entrance to the house is adorned with a corn-mill wheel, various baskets and firewood for cold winter days.*

Schlichtwegs bestechend: der bald dreihundertjährige Klapptisch mit Ofenbank und Holzstuhl. *Just charming: the folding table, nearly three hundred years old, with a bench around the stove and a wooden chair.*

Eine einfache „Brotzeit" auf einem alten Holztisch ist immer etwas Besonderes. *A simple snack at the old wooden table is always something special.*

Renato Balsamo schmückt Steine aus dem benachbarten Fluss mit ungewöhnlichen Gesichtern.
Renato Balsamo decorates stones from the nearby river with unusual faces.

Eagle's nest Adlerhorst

"No folklore architecture, please!" This was the owner's most urgent request, when he and his wife decided, more than thirty years ago, to build a holiday home on the most beautiful and sought-after hill above St Moritz. And so the house, designed by a friend of his youth, the Zurich architect Rolf Keller, became anything but a classic chalet. Large picture windows, "not those little traditional Engadine crenellated peepholes", allow a view of a panorama that sends many a guest into raptures. Majestically enthroned on the opposite side of the valley are the Piz Rosatsch, 3,134 metres high, and next to it the best-known mountain for skiing, the Piz Corvatsch, 3,451 metres above sea level. Spread out down below in the long, high-lying valley of the Inn lies the picturesque Silvaplaner lake. On the terrace side of the house, framed by thick wooden pillars that continue as marble pillars at ground level, the 3,099-metre Piz Albana and the Piz Julier, 300 metres higher, are delineated against the dark blue sky. "My local mountain," remarks the owner of the house with some pride. "I climb it every summer, at about 4 am, when the temperature is still bearable." A dash of Aspen, a dash of Hollywood and a little Swiss snowy landscape – this would be the simplest way of describing the style of this Engadine mountain house. The tall wide windows as well as the many wooden beams and pillars are reminiscent of the architecture at the American luxury winter sports resort, while the spectacular indoor swimming pool, the marble pillars, balustrades and bathrooms, as well as the gilded fittings and the Art Nouveau sculptures recall the glamour of the movie metropolis. And the whole eclectic interior has for thirty years been held together by a – constantly renewed – snow-white carpet. "A stone floor – that would be dreadful," the owner protests. "Where would be the comfort in that?" The entire setting in this grandly laid-out eagle's nest is subordinated to the incomparable view of the Engadine mountain range: a simple and movable oval seating area is linked by two wooden pillars in the salon, white piqué dining-room chairs match the modest glass table, study and library are furnished in contemporary style, and the modern kitchen leads to a long balcony which can also be reached from the guestroom. The tapering rooms directly under the roof are reserved for the owner, while the long swimming pool on the ground floor is open to all guests. But it can happen that the latter, gazing at the view of the mountain range bathed in the colours of the sunset through the huge windows, may forget that they are in the water …

„Nur ja keine Folklorearchitektur!" Dies war das wichtigste Anliegen des Hausherrn, als er mit seiner Frau vor über dreißig Jahren beschloss, am schönsten und von aller Welt begehrten Hügel oberhalb von St. Moritz eine Ferienresidenz bauen zu lassen. Und so ist das Haus, das sein Jugendfreund, der Architekt Rolf Keller aus Zürich, entwarf, alles andere als ein klassisches Chalet geworden. Große Fensterfronten, „keine kleinen traditionellen Engadiner Schießscharten", geben den Blick frei auf ein Panorama, das so manchen Gast in Verzückung geraten lässt. Majestätisch thronen sie auf der gegenüberliegenden Talseite, der Piz Rosatsch mit einer Höhe von 3134 Metern und daneben der bekannteste Skiberg, der Piz Corvatsch, auf 3451 Metern über dem Meeresspiegel. Tief unten im langen Hochtal des Inn liegt malerisch hingegossen der Silvaplanersee. Eingerahmt von dicken Holzsäulen, die sich im Erdgeschoss als Marmorsäulen fortsetzen, zeichnen sich auf der Terrassenseite des Hauses der 3099 Meter hohe Piz Albana und der drei hundert Meter höhere Piz Julier vom dunkelblauen Himmel ab. „Mein Hausberg", meint der Herr des Hauses nicht ohne Stolz, „den besteige ich jeden Sommer jeweils um vier Uhr in der Früh, wenn die Temperaturen noch erträglich sind." Ein bisschen Aspen, ein bisschen Hollywood und ein bisschen helvetische Schneelandschaft – so könnte man den Stil in diesem Engadiner Berghaus am einfachsten beschreiben: Die großen und hohen Fenster sowie die vielen Holzbalken und Säulen erinnern an die Architektur im amerikanischen Luxuswintersportort, während der spektakuläre Indoor-Swimmingpool, die Marmorsäulen, Balustraden und Bäder oder auch die vergoldeten

An unusual sight in the mountains: this wardrobe is clad in black leather. ***Ungewöhnlich in den Bergen: Die Garderobe ist in schwarzes Leder gekleidet.***

Armaturen und Jugendstilskulpturen an den Glamour der Filmmetropole mahnen. Und was das ganze eklektische Interieur schließlich zusammenhält, ist seit dreißig Jahren ein – immer wieder neu verlegter – schneeweißer Teppichboden. „Ein Steinboden – das wäre grauenhaft", ereifert sich der Hausbesitzer, „wo bleibt denn da die Gemütlichkeit?" Die gesamte Einrichtung in diesem großzügig angelegten Adlerhorst ist der unvergleichlichen Aussicht auf die Engadiner Bergketten untergeordnet: eine einfache und bewegliche ovale Sitzbank voller großer Kissen verbindet zwei Holzsäulen im Salon, weiße Pikee-Esszimmerstühle passen zum schlichten Glastisch, Büro und Bibliothek sind zeitgemäß ausgestattet, und die moderne Küche führt hinaus auf einen langen Balkon, der auch vom Gästezimmer erreichbar ist. Die abgeschrägten Räume direkt unter dem Dach sind dem Hausherrn vorbehalten, während das lange Schwimmbad im Erdgeschoss allen Gästen offen steht. Dabei kann es passieren, dass diese beim Anblick der ins Abendrot getauchten Bergketten vor dem riesengroßen Fenster vergessen, dass sie im Wasser sind ...

Bottom: Breathtaking: the view of the distant Corvatsch from the indoor swimming pool. ***Unten: Atemberaubend ist die Aussicht vom Indoor-Swimmingpool auf den Corvatsch in der Ferne.***

Right: A plentiful supply of art, marble and the colour white: everything is clear and bright. ***Rechts: Viel Kunst, viel Marmor und viel weiße Farbe: Hier sind Klarheit und Helligkeit angesagt.***

HELMUT NEWTON

Right: Elegance on a grand scale: in the salon, beams and a grand piano set the tone. ***Rechts: Großzügige Eleganz: Im Salon geben Balken und ein Flügel den Ton an.***

Impressive, but by no means massive, the chalet is enthroned at the very top of the Suvretta slope – built by Rolf Keller of Zurich. ***Imposant, aber keineswegs wuchtig thront das Chalet zuoberst am Suvrettahang – gebaut von Rolf Keller aus Zürich.***

Dining room with a special atmosphere. ***Esszimmer mit Flair.***

Evening mood: "Les Silènes" was built by the Megève architect Aldo Merlin. ***Abendstimmung: „Les Silènes" wurde vom Megèver Architekten Aldo Merlin gebaut.***

Right: They don't bark! The two dogs in the entrance hall are made of wood. ***Rechts: Sie bellen nicht, die beiden Holzhunde im Entree!***

Lawish comfort **Großzügige Gemütlichkeit**

"I'm not a hunter!" the owner laughingly admits, "but I just love everything to do with antlers, because they are so wonderfully decorative." And so, in his mountain house high above the French holiday resort of Megève, at the foot of the Mont Blanc massif in the Savoy Alps, sets of antlers of a great variety of animals are to be found, and in a multiplicity of forms and sizes: as chair legs and arms, lamp bases, mirrors, glass racks, bookshelves, chandeliers, chimneypieces or simply as humble candlesticks. These unusual "trophies" mainly date from the late nineteenth century; they were constructed with great skill by do-it-yourself enthusiasts from the country regions of France, Austria and Bavaria as well as Switzerland. But today, more than a hundred years later, the creation of these "horned" objects is again finding favour. And thus the owner of the chalet "Les Silènes" ("The Campions") in Megève was only recently able to find something quite novel for his original collection: two hide chairs framed with stag and elk antlers, created by the French artist Michel Haillard. These offbeat chairs, together with little antler side tables and a comfortable modern suede sofa on a colourful Turkish kilim rug, occupy the area under the high-beamed roof that is used as a living room. "We wanted a family house for us and our daughters," the owner, from Geneva, explains during the walk through the spacious chalet, with separate living and sleeping areas for the parents, the office and guests' area, the staff accommodation and a separate floor for the children, "but we also wanted a house for our friends, for parties and sociable evening groups." That this bright, comfortable wooden house with a view of Mont Charvin, the Aiguilles de Varan and the Aravis mountain ranges, can be used in so many ways, and that in particular the number of guests is of no importance, is shown by the carved inscription over the chimneypiece. "Dieu y donne l'accroissement" is inscribed on the broad beam, which once adorned a storehouse in Swiss Fribourg. A free translation might be: "Here God grants increase (of space)."

„Ein Jäger bin ich nicht !" gibt der Hausherr lachend zu, „aber ich liebe nun mal alles, was mit Geweihen zu tun hat, denn die sind so herrlich dekorativ." So finden sich denn in seinem Berghaus hoch über dem französischen Ferienort Megève am Fuße des Montblanc-Massivs in den savoyischen Alpen Geweihe verschiedenster Tierarten, und zwar in den unterschiedlichsten Formen und Größen: als Stuhllehnen, Tischbeine, Lampenfüße, Spiegel, Gläsergestelle, Bücherborde, Deckenleuchter, Kaminböcke oder einfach als schlichte Kerzenständer. Diese verfremdeten „Trophäen" stammen in ihrer Mehrzahl vom Ende des neunzehnten Jahrhunderts. Begeisterte Tüftler aus den ländlichen Regionen Frankreichs, Österreichs, Bayerns und auch der Schweiz haben sie mit viel Geschick zusammengebastelt. Doch auch heute, über hundert Jahre später, hat man wieder Gefallen gefunden am Kreieren dieser

Even the fire-dog is made of a set of antlers; in the foreground, an old Asian door acts as a table-top.
Sogar der Feuerbock ist ein Geweih; im Vordergrund eine alte asiatische Tür als Tischplatte.

Right: A perfect combination: the dining corner in the large salon.
Rechts: Perfekt kombiniert: die Essecke im großen Salon.

„gehörnten" Modelle. Und daher hat der Besitzer des Chalets „Les Silènes" („Leimkraut") in Megève für seine originelle Sammlung erst vor kurzem etwas ganz Neuartiges finden können: zwei Fellsessel eingerahmt mit Hirsch- und Elchgeweihen, die der französische Künstler Michel Haillard kreiert hat. Diese ausgefallenen Sessel zieren nun zusammen mit kleinen Geweih-Beistelltischchen neben bequemen modernen Wildledersofas auf einem farbenfrohen türkischen Kelim-Teppich den Teil unter dem hohen Balkendach, der als Wohnzimmer genutzt wird. „Wir wünschten uns ein Familienhaus für uns und unsere Töchter", erklärt der Genfer Hausherr beim Gang durch das geräumige Chalet mit dem separaten Eltern-, Wohn- und Schlafteil, dem Büro- und Gästetrakt, der Angestelltenwohnung und dem Stockwerk für die Kinder, „aber wir wollten auch ein Haus für unsere Freunde, für Parties und für gesellige Abendrunden." Dass sich das komfortable Holzhaus mit dem Blick auf den Mont Charvin, auf die Aiguilles de Varan und die Aravis-Bergkette vielseitig nutzen lässt und dabei insbesondere die Anzahl der Gäste ohne Bedeutung ist, zeigt der geschnitzte Spruch über dem Kamin. „Dieu y donne l'accroissement" steht auf dem breiten Balken, der einst einen Speicher im Schweizerischen Fribourg geschmückt hatte. Frei übersetzt könnte man sagen: „Gott gibt hier (Platz)Vermehrung".

In the centre of this living room, two horn chairs by Michel Haillard flank an old refectory table. ***Im Zentrum dieses Wohnzimmers flankieren zwei Hornsessel von Michel Haillard einen alten Refektoriumstisch.***

Old horn with a difference: as a rack for brandy bottles, a side table, a table lamp and a hanging lamp. ***Altes Horn einmal anders: als Schnapsgestell, Beistelltischchen, als Tischleuchte und Hängelampe.***

The Swiss craftsman in iron Bernhard Luginbühl designed this salon table for the living room.
Pflugtisch im Wohnzimmer: Der Schweizer Eisenplastiker Bernhard Luginbühl entwarf den Salontisch.

Bottom: The exterior of the chalet has been returned to its original appearance as in 1795. ***Unten: Das Chalet hat man äußerlich in seinen Originalzustand von 1795 zurückversetzt.***

Without extras: the guestroom in the "Gruebehus".
Ohne Extras: das Gästezimmer im „Gruebehus".

Kunststücke

Alles was alt und ehrwürdig ist, Geschichten erzählen könnte und Traditionen in sich birgt, gefällt dem gebürtigen Basler, der sich deshalb auch vor Jahren ins „Gruebehus", ein über zweihundert Jahre altes Bauernhaus im Saanenland am Fuße des Horneggli verliebte. Und mit der selben Leidenschaft, mit der er sich um seine große Sammlung alter Autos gekümmert hat, widmete er sich auch seinem neu erworbenen Berghaus im Berner Oberland. Nachdem er sich gründlich mit der Stilkunde der Bauernhäuser aus der Gegend beschäftigt hatte, ließ der neue Besitzer das „Gruebehus" bis auf die Kellermauern abtragen und in seine Einzelteile zerlegen – wobei jeder Balken minutiös nummeriert wurde. Aus fast dreihundert Stämmen besteht ein solcher traditioneller Bauernhof aus dem Saanenland, das Gebälk ragt ein Stück aus der Außenwand hervor, und kennzeichnend sind auch die beiden steilen Treppen links und rechts an der Vorderfront, die jeweils in die beiden „Lauben" hinaufführen. Ursprünglich gab es auch im „Gruebehus" zwei Stuben: links einen separaten Teil für die Eltern und rechts den für den ältesten Sohn. Über die beiden Treppen gelangte man damals in die entsprechenden Schlafstuben. Heute dienen die einstigen unbeheizten Lauben als Ess- und Schlafzimmer. Der Hausherr, der alles „Unehrliche" in einem Haus verabscheut, hat sich in seinem neu zusammengesetzten Domizil für klare Linien entschieden – und für moderne Kunst. Das große Wohnzimmer mit der einfachen Holzdecke, das aus zwei kleineren Stuben entstanden ist, schmücken Werke von befreundeten Schweizer Künstlern wie Jean Tinguely, Bernhard Luginbühl oder Niki de Saint Phalle. An den Holzwänden hängen Werke zeitgenössischer Künstler oder die traditionellen Scherenschnittbilder aus dem benachbarten Rougemont. Die Möbel sind entweder gradlinig modern oder einfache, antike Bauernmöbel aus der Gegend. Die neue Hauptachse im „Gruebehus" bildet eine moderne Stahltreppe, die das umgebaute Kellergeschoss mit den Zimmern unter dem Giebel verbindet. Konsequent hat der Hausherr alle Details getreu den Bräuchen im Saanenland restaurieren oder neu schmieden lassen. So ist jedes Scharnier, jedes Türband, jeder Griff, jedes Schloss ein kleines Kunstwerk für sich.

Achievements

Everything that is old and venerable, that could tell a story and contains traditions, appeals to the Basle-born owner of the "Gruebehus". He fell in love with the more than 200-year-old farmhouse in the Saanenland, at the foot of the Horneggli, years ago. And with the same passion which he has applied to his large collection of old motor cars, he has also dedicated himself to his newly acquired mountain house in the Bernese Oberland. After thoroughly studying the stylistics of local farmhouses, the new owner of the "Gruebehus" had it dismantled right down to the cellar walls and reduced to its component parts, each beam being meticulously numbered. A traditional Saanenland farmhouse such as this is made from nearly 300 tree-trunks, the rafters project somewhat from the exterior walls, and also typical are the two steep staircases at the left and right of the front of the house, which each lead up to the two "bowers". Originally there were also two parlours in the "Gruebehus": on the left a separate one for the parents, and on the right, one for the eldest son. At that time the two staircases led to the corresponding bedrooms. Today the former unheated "bowers" serve as dining rooms and bedrooms. The master of the house, who abhors anything "dishonest" in a house, in putting his home back together again has decided in favour of "clear

lines" – and of modern art. The large living room with the simple wooden ceiling, which was constructed from two smaller rooms, is decorated with works by Swiss artists, friends of the owner, such as Jean Tinguely, Bernhard Luginbühl and Niki de Saint Phalle. On the wooden walls hang works by contemporary artists and traditional silhouettes from nearby Rougemont. The furniture consists of both modern pieces, in straight lines, and simple antique peasant pieces from the local area. The new main axis in the "Gruebehus" is formed by a modern steel staircase, which links the rebuilt cellar level with the rooms below the gables. With total consistency, the owner has restored all the details in keeping with Saanenland tradition, or had them newly reconstructed. Thus every door fitting, every hinge, every handle, every lock is a little work of art in itself.

Links: Leichtigkeit des Seins: Albert Obrist entschied sich für eine Stahltreppe als Verbindungsglied der Stockwerke. *Left: Lightness of being: Albert Obrist decided on a steel staircase as a connecting link between floors.*

Oben: Steinplatten, Chromstahl und altes Holz machen die Küche pflegeleicht und wohnlich zugleich. *Top: Stone slabs, chromed steel and old wood make the kitchen easy to clean and welcoming at the same time.*

Rechts: Der Aufgang zum Glück: eine „Laube" mit steiler Treppe. *Right: Ascent to happiness: a "bower" with steep steps.*

Stillleben im Saanenland: Klapptisch und Hocker sind dreihundert Jahre alt. *Still life in the Saanenland: the folding table and stool are three hundred years old.*

Moderne Kunst auf altem Holz: Der Hausherr liebt klare Aussagen. *Modern art on old wood: the owner likes clear statements.*

Idylle im Berner Oberland.
Idyllic place in the Bernese Oberland.

Hunting fever Jagdfieber

Gräfliche Jagdgründe

Der Blick von der Terrasse könnte berauschender nicht sein: Vor uns liegen von der Abendsonne beleuchtet die Almsee-Berge, also der Nordrand des Toten Gebirges, und links erhebt sich majestätisch der Große Priel, der höchste Berg Oberösterreichs. „Abgesehen vom Dachstein natürlich", werden wir schmunzelnd belehrt, „aber den müssen wir uns mit der Steiermark teilen." Die einladende Terrasse gehört zum „Jagdhaus über'm Springbach", einem charmanten Holzhaus, das 1908 im damals typischen Landhausstil errichtet worden ist. Die Erbauer – Olivier Graf Lamezan-Salins und dessen Frau Mathilde, eine geborene Edle von Hardtmuth – waren Vorfahren des heutigen Hausherrn. „Den Namen bekam unser Jagdhaus von dem kleinen Wildbach mit Wasserfall, der gleich hier unten vorbeifließt," erläutert der Enkel der Bauherrn, der jeweils zwischen Mitte September und Mitte Oktober mit seinen Freunden zur Hirschbrunft in sein Familienhaus fährt. Gelegen ist der Jagdtreffpunkt auf einer kleinen verwunschenen Lichtung am sogenannten „Miraberg" in der Hetzau, einem Jagdparadies im Almtal. „Bei uns jagen nur die Männer – Hochwild, also Rot-, Gams- und Rehwild. Die Trophäen im Salon sind übrigens meine besten Hirsche aus über vierzig Jahren Jagd in Grünau." Die Hirschgeweihe auf der Esszimmerwand hingegen stammen aus einem slowenischen Familienbesitz, der 1945 enteignet wurde. Das „Jagdhaus über'm Springbach" verfügt zusätzlich zu den beiden großen Räumen, die mit alten Öfen aus der Hardtmuth-Kachelofen-Fabrik ausgestattet sind, über fünf geräumige Schlafzimmer und zwei abgetrennte, nur von außen begehbare Räume – „für einen Diener und zwei Jäger". Eingerichtet ist das Jagdjuwel mit Möbeln aus der Biedermeierzeit und einfachen Holzmöbeln, die von einheimischen Tischlern gefertigt wurden. „Bemerkenswert sind in unserem Haus auch die Wasserklos", fügt der Hausherr nicht ohne Stolz an, „die stammen noch aus dem Jahr 1908."

Links: Das „Jagdhaus über'm Springbach" in der Hetzau in Oberösterreich. *Left: The "Jagdhaus über'm Springbach" in the Hetzau district in Upper Austria.*

Der prächtige Ofen im Salon stammt von der familieneigenen Hardtmuth-Kachelofen-Fabrik. *The superb stove in the salon comes from Hardtmuth, the family-owned ceramic stove factory.*

Hochwildtrophäen kombiniert mit Stühlen und einem traditionellen Kugelofen. *Game trophies combined with chairs and a traditional ceramic oven.*

Noble hunting grounds

The view from the terrace could not be more enchanting. In front of us, lit by the evening sun, lie the Almsee mountains, the northern edge of the Totengebirge, and to the left the Grosse Priel, the highest mountain in Upper Austria, rises majestically. "Apart from the Dachstein, of course," we are told with a smile, "we have to share that with Styria." The welcoming terrace belongs to the "Jagdhaus über'm Springbach", a charming wooden house built in 1908 in the country-house style of that period. Those who built it – Olivier Graf Lamezan-Salins and his wife Mathilde, née Edle von Hardtmuth – were the ancestors of the present owner. "Our hunting lodge got its name from the little mountain stream with a waterfall, that flows past directly below us," explains the grandson of the first owner, who regularly travels to his family house with his friends between mid-September and mid-October, when the stags are in rut. The meeting point for hunters is a little isolated clearing on the so-called Miraberg in the Hetzau district, a hunting paradise in the Almtal. "Here only the men hunt – the larger game animals, red deer, chamois and roe-deer. The trophies in the salon, by the way, are from my best stags from more than forty years of

hunting in Grünau." The noble, mighty stag antlers on the wooden walls of the dining room on the other hand come from a Slovenian family property that was expropriated in 1945. The "Jagdhaus über'm Springbach" has, in addition to the two large rooms furnished with old stoves from the Hardtmuth tiled stove factory, five spacious bedrooms and two separate rooms, accessible only from the outside – "for a servant and two huntsmen". This jewel of an Austrian hunting lodge is furnished with pieces from the Biedermeier period and simple wooden furniture made by local craftsmen. "The lavatories are worth noticing, too, in this house," adds the owner, not without some pride. "They go back to 1908."

Links: Schlicht gehalten sind auch die Schlafzimmer des Jagdhauses von 1908. *Left: Also modest in style are the bedroom furnishings of the hunting lodge, built in 1908.*

Oben: In dieser Stube treffen sich die Jagdgesellschaften von Mitte September bis Mitte Oktober. *Top: In this room, hunting parties meet from mid-September to mid-October.*

Impressive: the "Promegg House", more than one hundred years old, on the Wolfgangsee. ***Imposant: das über hundert Jahre alte „Promegg Haus" am Wolfgangsee.***

Right: Elegant and countrified: the entry.
Rechts: Elegant und ländlich zugleich: das Entree.

Country house with an air of grandezza

"Haus Promegg" has become a household name, in Austria and Holland as well as in England. A byword for hospitality, style, tradition and carefree summer days. This old hunting property high above the Wolfgangsee is the Austrian holiday home of Robert and Susanna van Maasdijk – a cosmopolitan couple, native to Holland and Sweden and resident in England. These two jetsetters love to welcome guests from all over the world to "Haus Promegg" and to spoil them. The impressive yellow-painted villa, built in 1897 by Baron Vincent van Tujll van Seerooskerken, the great-grandfather of the present owner, has all the necessary qualities to make you feel at ease: an entrance hall that also serves as a library, a cosy hunting room, completely panelled in wood, with a number of trophies, a salon of rural elegance, a dining room with the lake view of one's dreams, various administrative rooms and splendid bedrooms for nineteen people. "If there should be more, there's no problem," says the hostess. "We simply use the hunting lodge next door, as well, where there's room for another eleven people." Over the years Robert and Susanna van Maasdijk have provided "Haus Promegg" with contemporary comfort. "Anything that we have renovated or replaced was chosen to look as though it has always been here," says the lady of the house. "The fabrics are not glamorous and elegant, but mostly simple Tissu Colbert fabrics from Salzburg, the furniture, with the exception of a few French antique pieces, is all Austrian and has been in this house for over a hundred years, the newly bought beds are antique, hand-painted wooden beds in country style, and the sofas and chairs are covered with suede and chamois leather in keeping with the style of the house." Not to be forgotten are the four newly installed bathrooms, "because only three bathrooms for nineteen people seemed to be cutting it rather fine". At "Haus Promegg", apart from the stylish country environment and perfect service – eight members of staff are on duty during the summer – even more is offered. "We love competitions and games of all kinds," confides the hostess. "Apart from hunting, we play bridge, backgammon, rummy, organize table-tennis or tennis matches on our own court, and in summer we have swimming competitions." Even after these sporting activities, Robert and Susanna van Maasdijk prove themselves to be accomplished hosts: lunch is served on a beautifully decorated table in the dining room of the boathouse. "There is easily room for twenty people, but to make room for the table we had to move 'Henriette', our rowing boat ..."

Landsitz mit Grandezza

Das „Haus Promegg" ist zu einem Begriff geworden. In Österreich und Holland genauso wie in England. Ein Begriff für Gastfreundschaft, für Stil, Tradition und für unbeschwerte Sommertage. Ist dieses alte Jagdanwesen hoch über dem Wolfgangsee doch das österreichische Feriendomizil von Robert und Susanna van Maasdijk – eines kosmopolitischen, in England ansässigen und aus Holland und Schweden stammenden Ehepaars. Diese beiden Jetsetter lieben es, Gäste aus aller Welt bei sich zu beherbergen und zu verwöhnen. Die imposante, gelb getünchte Villa, die 1897 von Baron Vincent van Tujll van Seerooskerken, dem Urgroßvater des heutigen Besitzers, gebaut wurde, weist die notwendigen Voraussetzungen auf, um sich wohl zu fühlen: eine Eingangshalle, die auch als Bibliothek dient, ein gemütliches, ganz in Holz verkleidetes Jagdzimmer, einen ländlich-eleganten Salon, ein Esszimmer mit Traumaussicht auf den See, diverse Wirtschaftsräume und Schlafzimmer für neunzehn Personen. „Wenn wir mehr sind, ist dies auch kein Problem", meint die Gastgeberin, „dann benutzen wir zusätzlich unser Jägerhaus gleich nebenan, in dem nochmals elf Personen Platz finden." Im Laufe der Jahre haben Robert und Susanna van Maasdijk das „Haus Promegg" mit zeitgemäßem Komfort versehen. „Was immer wir renoviert oder ersetzt haben, wurde so gewählt, dass es ausschaut, als wenn es schon immer hier gewesen wäre, die Stoffe sind nicht glamourös und elegant, sondern meist einfache ‚Tissu Colbert'-Stoffe aus Salzburg, die Möbel sind mit Ausnahme einiger weniger französischer Antiquitäten alle aus Österreich und schon seit über hundert Jahren in diesem Haus, die neu erworbenen Betten sind antike, handbemalte Holzbetten, und die Sofas und Stühle sind passend zum Stil des Hauses in Wildleder und Gamsfell bezogen." Nicht zu vergessen sind die vier neu installierten Badezimmer, „denn nur drei Badestuben für neunzehn Menschen – das war etwas knapp". Den Gästen wird im „Haus Promegg" neben stilvollem Country-Ambiente und perfektem Service – acht Helfer sind im Sommer im Einsatz – noch einiges mehr geboten. „Wir lieben Wettkämpfe und Spiele diversester Art", gesteht die Hausfrau, „neben der Jagd, spielen wir Bridge, Backgammon oder veranstalten Pingpong-Matches." Auch später zeigen sich Robert und Susanna van Maasdijk als formvollendete Gastgeber: Das Mittagessen wird an einer wunderschön gedeckten Tafel im Speisezimmer des Bootshauses serviert. „Zwanzig Personen haben leicht Platz, doch für den Tisch musste ‚Henriette', unser Ruderboot, weichen ..."

Top left: The painted furniture comes from Holland and dates from about 1750. ***Oben links: Das bemalte Mobiliar stammt aus Holland und datiert um die Zeit von 1750.***

Top right: This salon with its carved woodwork is a meeting-place for young and old. ***Oben rechts: Der Salon mit den Boiserien ist Treffpunkt für Jung und Alt.***

The stairwell in the entrance was constructed by Dutch joiners and also serves as a library. ***Das Treppenhaus im Entree wurde von holländischen Schreinern gefertigt und dient auch als Bibliothek.***

Großwildjagd mit Allure

Den Leoparden hat die Hausherrin als Neunzehnjährige in Kenia auf einer Safari geschossen, den Löwen hat ihr Ehemann erlegt, und das Nashorn ist eine Trophäe ihrer Mutter. Dass die Bewohner dieses Berghauses in Kitzbühel im österreichischen Tirol leidenschaftliche Jäger sind, dafür gibt es eindeutige Zeichen. Überall trifft man in diesem imposanten Anwesen, das in den späten fünfziger Jahren durch den Architekten Ernst von Demar für die Familie Auersberg entworfen worden ist, auf ungewöhnliche Trophäen – von afrikanischen Büffeln bis zu einheimischen Böcken. Doch dass hier zusätzlich mit großer Eleganz und stilvoll gelebt wird, ist ebenfalls unübersehbar. Aus den verschiedensten Winkeln der Welt stammen die exquisiten Antiquitäten und Familienstücke. So schmückte der antike Aubusson-Teppich im Salon einst das Wiener Elternhaus der Hausherrin, der Kamin gehörte in ein Pariser „Hotel Particulier", und die Fayancen im Esszimmer wurden in ganz Europa zusammengetragen. Den Blick für das Besondere hat auch die Hausfrau geerbt. Ist die Kunsthistorikerin aus London, wo sie zu Hause ist, doch über die Landesgrenzen hinaus bekannt als Expertin und Händlerin für gesuchte Meisterzeichnungen aus dem sechzehnten und siebzehnten Jahrhundert. So erstaunt es auch nicht, dass in ihrer Tiroler Bergresidenz die Wände mit ungewöhnlichen Malereien, Zeichnungen und Kupferstichen geschmückt sind. Die Bibliothek ist der Familienraum schlechthin. Dieser mit Fichtenholz ausgelegte urgemütliche Raum gleich neben dem formelleren Salon ist dekoriert mit zahlreichen Jagdtrophäen und unzähligen Büchern. Es sind vor allem klassische französische Schriften, unter anderem von Voltaire und Rousseau, aber auch Kunst- und Geschichtsbücher, die die Hausherrin hier in aller Abgeschiedenheit mit viel Muße studieren kann.

Big game hunting in style

The leopard was shot by the lady of the house when on safari in Kenya as a nineteen-year-old, the lion was killed by her husband, and the rhino is a trophy of her mother's. That the occupants of this mountain dwelling in Kitzbühel, in the Austrian Tyrol, are passionate hunters, is clear from the evidence. Everywhere in this impressive property, which was designed in the late 1950s for the Auersberg family by the architect Ernst von Demar, one comes across unusual trophies – from African buffalo to local deer. But in addition, it is equally obvious that life is conducted here with great elegance and style. The exquisite antiques and family heirlooms come from the most varied corners of the earth. The antique Aubusson carpet in the salon, for example, once graced the Vienna house of the lady owner's parents, the chimneypiece came from a hôtel particulier in Paris, and the faience in the dining room was collected from all over Europe. The owner has also inherited a taste for the unusual. An art historian living in London, she is known beyond national boundaries as an expert and dealer in sought-after old master drawings of the sixteenth and seventeenth centuries. So it is not surprising that in her Tyrolean mountain home the walls are adorned with rare paintings, drawings and engravings.The library is, quite simply, the family room. This immensely comfortable room, with its sprucewood panelling, right next to the more formal salon, is decorated with a number of hunting trophies and countless books. The vast majority of these are classic French texts, including those by Voltaire and Rousseau, but also art and history books, which the mistress of the house can study here at her leisure in total seclusion.

Rechts: Erlegt und ausgestreckt: Den Leoparden schoss die Hausherrin als Neunzehnjährige in Kenia. *Right: The leopard was shot in Kenya by the mistress of the house when she was nineteen.*

Für die Familie Auersberg entworfen und gemalt: Auch die Eingangshalle ist in diversen Grautönen gehalten. *Designed and painted for the Auersberg family: the entrance hall is also in several shades of grey.*

Der Löwe, der die alte Bank im Entree schmückt, ist eine der zahlreichen Trophäen in diesem Jagdchalet in Kitzbühel. *The lion who adorns the old bench at the entrance is one of the many trophies at this hunting chalet in Kitzbühel.*

Verborgene Wasserspiele: Unterhalb des Hauses liegt der romantische Swimmingpool. *Hidden water games: below the house lies the romantic swimming pool.*

Blauschattierungen: Haupteingang ins blumengeschmückte Bergdomizil. *Shades of blue: main entrance to the flower-decked mountain residence.*

„Jagdstudien" kann man sich auch in der Bibliothek widmen. *In the library one can dedicate oneself to "hunting studies".*

Blick ins elegante Speisezimmer mit Familienmöbeln. *A view of the elegant dining room with family furniture.*

In Holz gewandet: der Salon sowie im Hintergrund die Bibliothek. Einen wichtigen Platz nimmt das Porträt des Karl-Emil von Fürstenberg ein, dem Großvater des heutigen Besitzers. *Clad in wood: the salon as well as the library in the background. A prominent position is occupied by the portrait of Karl-Emil von Fürstenberg, the grandfather of the present owner.*

Im Zeichen von Hubertus

In Oberösterreich im Salzkammergut, ganz in der Nähe von Bad Ischl, wo Kaiser Franz Josef und seine Frau Elisabeth von Bayern, genannt Sissi, jeweils zur Jagd- und Badesaison residierten, befindet sich der „Hubertushof", die zweihundertfünfzig Jahre alte Sommerresidenz derer von und zu Fürstenberg. Am Wolfgangsee ist der schöne Hof gelegen, den Karl-Emil von Fürstenberg, einst österreichischer Botschafter am Zarenhof von Niklaus II., Ende des vorletzten Jahrhunderts von seinem Vater geerbt hat. „Gebaut wurde das Jagdhaus im Jahr 1758 für einen Florentiner Noblen, den Duca de Boiano", erzählt der heutige Besitzer Prinz Egon von und zu Fürstenberg, „und zwar von einem italienischen Architekten. Die Frau des Herzogs war eine passionierte Jägerin, doch sie wurde unglücklicherweise getötet, und er verkaufte dann den Hof an meinen Urgroßvater Maximilian, der ihn an seinen zweiten Sohn Karl-Emil vererbte." Karl-Emils Sohn Tassilo von Fürstenberg, der Vater von Egon und Ira, wiederum machte den malerisch gelegenen „Hubertushof" während der vierziger und fünfziger Jahre des letzten Jahrhunderts zum sommerlichen Treffpunkt für internationale Politiker und Vertreter der High Society. Von Franklin D. Roosevelt bis Winston Churchill, von John F. Kennedy bis Orson Welles, vom König von Spanien bis zu Herbert von Karajan trafen sich die Großen, Schönen und Wichtigen dieser Welt in diesem bezaubernden Anwesen. Sie alle bewunderten die unzähligen Geweihe, die noch heute die Wände über dem Holztäfer im großen Salon zieren. Die meisten stammen von Karl-Emil von Fürstenberg, der seine Jagdtrophäen aus Ungarn, Russland und dem Sudan heimbrachte. Zwei riesengroße Elefantenstoßzähne erinnern in der Zimmerecke an seine Großwildjagdzeiten in Kenia. „Auch mein Vater Tassilo war ein großer Jäger", erzählt der heutige Besitzer, „und gleichzeitig auch ein begeisterter Fischer. Im Sommer konnte man ihn stundenlang mitten in der Traun, unserem benachbarten Fluss, stehend beim Forellenfangen beobachten." Verändert wurde im prachtvollen Hof, der unter dem Zeichen des Heiligen Hubertus, des Schutzpatrons der Jäger steht, nur Äußerliches. „Mein Vater ließ Tennisplätze, ein kleines Restaurant und einen Minigolfplatz für die vielen Gäste anlegen", erläutert der heutige Hausherr, der mit seiner Couture-Kollektion international tätig ist und sich auch in Rom, Paris, New York und Rio zu Hause fühlt. Mit Begeisterung erinnert sich der Kosmopolit aber noch heute an „die vielen herrlichen Salzburger Sommertage mit meinen Verwandten". Das Haus ist ein klassisches dreistöckiges Jagdhaus, eidottergelb bemalt, gradlinig und unverschnörkelt. Vierundzwanzig Zimmer zählt der Hof, auf zwei Etagen verteilt. Zehn Badezimmer wurden hinzugefügt, außerdem ein Zentralheizungssystem eingebaut, sodass sich heute Familie und Gästeschar auch von den „so überaus romantischen" Wintertagen am Wolfgangsee bezaubern lassen können. Dann trifft man sich in der holzgetäfelten Bibliothek mit den geschnitzten Möbeln, dem Spieltisch und den antiken Büchern, die seit jeher zwei den Raum umspannende Gestelle bewohnen. Viele von ihnen stammen noch von Lady Hamilton, der Mutter von Karl-Emils Ehefrau Maria. Das wichtigste Buch aber liegt in einer Ecke des eleganten Salons: Es ist das goldene Gästebuch, das seit 1889 alle Unterschriften der Geladenen auf dem „Hubertushof" sammelt.

In the tradition of St Hubert

In the Salzkammergut in Upper Austria, near Bad Ischl, where Emperor Franz Josef and his wife Elisabeth of Bavaria, known as Sissi, stayed during the hunting and spa season, is the "Hubertushof", the two-hundred-and-fifty-year-old summer residence of the von und zu Fürstenberg family. This beautiful house on the Wolfgangsee was inherited at the end of the penultimate century from his father by Karl-Emil von Fürstenberg, once the Austrian ambassador to the court of Tsar Nicholas II. "It was built as a hunting lodge in 1758 for a Florentine nobleman, the Duca de Boiano", recounts the present owner, Prince Egon von und zu Fürstenberg, "and by an Italian architect. The duke's wife was a passionate huntress, but unfortunately she was killed, and he then sold the house to my great-grandfather Maximilian, who left it to his second son, Karl-Emil." During the 1940s and 1950s, Karl-Emil's son Tassilo von Fürstenberg, the father of Egon and Ira, in his turn made the picturesque "Hubertushof" into a summer meeting-place for international politicians and high society. From Franklin D. Roosevelt to Winston Churchill, from John F. Kennedy to Orson Welles, from the King of Spain to Herbert von Karajan, the great and the good of the world met in this enchanting environment. They all admired the countless sets of antlers that today still adorn the walls above the wooden panelling in the grand salon. Most of these were provided by Karl-Emil von Fürstenberg, who brought home his hunting trophies from Hungary, Russia and the Sudan. Two gigantic elephant tusks in the corner of the room are a memento of his big-game hunting in Kenya. "My father Tassilo was a great hunter too," relates the present owner, "and also an enthusiastic angler. In the summer he could be seen standing in our local river, the Traun, for hours at a time catching trout." Only external details have been altered in the splendid building, which is dedicated to St Hubert, the patron saint of hunters. "My father had tennis courts built, and also a small restaurant and a minigolf area for the many visitors", explains the present owner, who runs an international couture collection and feels at home in Rome, Paris, New York and Rio. But this cosmopolitan figure still remembers with enthusiasm "the many glorious Salzburg summer days with my relatives". The house is a classic three-storey hunting lodge, painted in egg-yolk yellow, with straight lines and without ornamentation. There are twenty-four rooms distributed on two floors. Ten bathrooms were added and a central heating system installed, so that today the crowds of relatives and guests can allow themselves to be enthralled by the "so very romantic" winter days by the Wolfgangsee. Then everyone meets in the wood-panelled library with the carved furniture, the gaming tale and antiquarian books, which have always been kept in the two ranges of shelving that span the room. Many of them were the property of Lady Hamilton, the mother of Karl-Emil's wife Maria. But the most important book of all lies in a corner of the elegant salon. It is the golden guest-book, in which since 1889 the signatures of all the guests of the "Hubertushof" have been collected.

Die Geweihe stehen Spalier: Der lange Gang führt zu den Schlafzimmern. *Antlers line the route: the long corridor leads to the bedrooms.*

Den großen Salon schmücken alte Ledersessel, ein Kachelofen, Memorabilias und Jagdtrophäen aus Ungarn, Russland und dem Sudan. *The large salon is adorned by old leather chairs, a ceramic stove, memorabilia and hunting trophies from Hungary, Russia and the Sudan.*

Das Schlafzimmer des Hausherrn ist ländlich elegant eingerichtet. *The owner's bedroom is furnished in elegant country style.*

Sie verfolgen einen bis unters Dach: Auch im dritten Stockwerk findet sich eine ungewöhnliche Jagdbeute.
They pursue one even to the underside of the roof: the third floor also boasts an unusual hunting trophy.

Im achtzehnten Jahrhundert gebaut: der „Hubertushof" von Prinz Egon von und zu Fürstenberg am Wolfgangsee. *Built in the eighteenth century: the "Hubertushof" on the Wolfgangsee, owned by Prince Egon von und zu Fürstenberg.*

“Zeitgeist” Zeitgeist

Engadiner Impressionen
Impressions of the Engadine

Fenster sind offen
Stäubchen auf sonnigem Strahl
Tanzende Geister.

Windows are open
Specks of dust on a sunbeam
Dancing spirits.

Das Haus am Flusse
Verschneite Vogelbeere
Die Scheune voll Klang.

The house by the stream
Snow-covered rowanberries
The barn full of sounds.

Links: Eine spektakuläre Steinrampe führt in den hohen Scheunenraum und durch die rote geteilte Flügeltür ins Innere des Hauses. *Left: A spectacular stone ramp leads to the high barn space and through the red divided double doors into the house's interior.*

Oben: Raffinierte Verbindung: In den „Talvo", die Scheune des alten Engadiner Hauses, wurde für einen Gästetrakt, einschließlich Bäder, und die Stromversorgung eine moderne „Box" gebaut. *Top: Sophisticated connection: in the "Talvo", the barn belonging to the old Engadine house, a "box" was built to accommodate a section for guests, including bathrooms and electricity supply.*

Geschichten fließen
Hinunter zum Schwarzen Meer
Ewig durch die Zeit.
Stories are flowing
Through time and eternity
Down to the Black Sea.

Links: Schlichte Wohligkeit: Alle Betten in diesem Haus sind mit feinstem gestärkten weißen und sandfarbenen Leinen bezogen. *Left: Unpretentious comfort: all the beds in this house are furnished with the finest starched white and sand-coloured linen.*

Oben: Alles original: Wie das Patrizierhaus selbst stammt auch das Mobiliar in der Bibliothek aus dem Jahr 1642. *Top: verything original: like this aristocratic house itself, the library furniture dates from 1642.*

Rechts: Weniger ist mehr: Hier spricht ein altes Haus mit seinen klaren Linien ganz für sich allein. *Right: Less is more: here an old house with its clear lines simply speaks for itself.*

Eine Steintreppe führt hinauf in eine Gästekammer. *A stone staircase leads up to a guestroom.*

Klare Formen, satte Farben: Blick vom „Sulèr", dem Gang, in die getäfelte „Stüva bela", den Hauptwohnraum. *Clearly defined forms, rich colours: the view from the "Sulèr", the passage, of the panelled "Stüva bela", the main living room.*

Art in the Alps

Enthroned up high, firmly anchored to the mountain above the Alpine community of Saanen, the Lambert family house has something solid, something peaceful and good-humoured about it. "My brother-in-law, Baron Léon Lambert, who built the house nearly fifteen years ago, didn't want anything old or reproduction," explains the present owner, Baroness Marion Lambert. "He was a well-known collector of contemporary art and so he felt that his house in the mountains should also be rooted in the present." The Belgian art connoisseur therefore commissioned the American architect Edward Knowles, a friend of many artists, who among other things also designed Boston City Hall and Lowell Nesbitt's studio. The result is a large, unpretentious mountain house, which captivates the visitor through its straight lines, its truth to its materials, and its harmony. But the Belgian was only to enjoy the fulfilment of his dream for a mere three months. After his death, his brother and his sister-in-law, Baroness Marion Lambert, took over the property. Not only forms and colours, but everything out of the ordinary arouses Marion Lambert's curiosity. Years ago – thanks to her children, as she emphasizes – she discovered a great love for furniture and furnishings from the 1940s and 1950s. Dutch by birth, she is also a passionate art collector, and so, looking down on chairs by Jean Prouvé and Jean Royère, furniture by Charles and Ray Eames, and lamps by Serge Mouille, the many white walls are now adorned with breathtaking works by contemporary artists. "I love living in a modern environment – it's so endlessly calm and peaceful," says the Baroness, who has excellent connections with the international art scene. Her Gstaad home houses works inspiring enthusiasm, paintings by Francesco Clemente, Philip Taffe, Sandro Chia, Christopher Wool and Ross Bleckner, and photography by Cindy Sherman, Robert Frank and Robert Mapplethorpe. So it is more of a museum for living in? A mountain home as a *Gesamtkunstwerk*? "For us it is above all a place where we can relax wonderfully," says Marion Lambert. For her relaxing breaks she appreciates the library which she has set up on the intermediate floor above the salon, and where, with professional meticulousness and passion, she has archived her innumerable books about photography. They all document in seamless fashion the collection of contemporary photography that she has brought together in her role as art connoisseur.

Mountain house near Gstaad, designed by the American architect Edward Knowles.
Trutzburg in der Nähe von Gstaad, entworfen vom amerikanischen Architekten Edward Knowles.

Art and design mecca: Baroness Marion Lambert collects paintings, photographs and choice items of furniture of the 1940s and 1950s. ***Kunst- und Design-Mekka: Baronin Marion Lambert sammelt Malerei, Fotografie und erlesene Möbelstücke aus den vierziger und fünfziger Jahren des letzten Jahrhunderts.***

Kunst in den Bergen

Wie es da oben fest verankert über der Berggemeinde Saanen am Berg thront, das Haus der Familie Lambert, hat etwas Solides, etwas Friedliches, etwas Gutmütiges an sich. „Mein Schwager, Baron Léon Lambert, der das Haus vor bald fünfzehn Jahren bauen ließ, mochte nichts Altes und nichts Nachgemachtes“, erklärt die heutige Besitzerin Baronin Marion Lambert, „er war ein bekannter Sammler von Gegenwartskunst und daher der Ansicht, dass auch sein Haus in den Bergen in der Gegenwart wurzeln sollte.“ So verpflichtete der belgische Kunstkenner den amerikanischen Architekten Edward Knowles, einen Freund vieler Künstler, der unter anderem auch die Boston City Hall und das Studio von Lowell Nesbitt entworfen hat. Entstanden ist ein großes einfaches Berghaus, das durch seine Gradlinigkeit, seine Materialtreue und durch seine Harmonie besticht. Doch der Belgier durfte seinen Traum bloß drei Monate genießen. Nach seinem Tode übernahmen der Bruder und dessen Frau, Baronin Marion Lambert, den Besitz. Nicht nur Formen und Farben, alles, was aus dem Rahmen fällt, macht Marion Lambert neugierig. So hat sie auch schon vor Jahren – dank ihren Kindern, wie sie betont – ihre große Liebe zu Möbeln und Wohngegenständen aus den vierziger und fünfziger Jahren des letzten Jahrhunderts entdeckt. Und da die gebürtige Holländerin ebenfalls passionierte Kunstsammlerin ist, zieren nun neben Sesseln von Jean Prouvé, Stühlen von Jean Royère, Möbeln von Charles und Ray Eames sowie Lampen von Serge Mouille atemberaubende Werke zeitgenössischer Künstler die vielen weißen Wände. „Ich liebe es, in einem modernen zeitgemäßen Ambiente zu wohnen, es ist so unendlich friedlich, so ruhig“, sagt die Frau mit den exzellenten Verbindungen zur internationalen Kunstszene. In ihrem Gstaader Domizil begeistern Bilder von Francesco Clemente, Philip Taffe, Sandro Chia, Christopher Wool und Ross Bleckner, Fotokunst von Cindy Sherman, Robert Frank und Robert Mapplethorpe. Also eher ein Museum zum Wohnen? Ein Berghaus als Gesamtkunstwerk? „Es ist für uns vor allem ein Ort, an dem wir herrlich entspannen können“, sagt Marion Lambert. Für ihre Ruhepausen schätzt sie die Bibliothek, die sie auf dem Zwischenstockwerk über dem Salon eingerichtet hat, und wo sie mit Akribie und Leidenschaft ihre unzähligen Fotobände archiviert. Sie alle dokumentieren lückenlos die Sammlung von zeitgenössischer Fotografie, die die Kunstkennerin zusammengetragen hat.

In the stairwell one can admire works by Ross Bleckner and Andy Warhol. ***Im Treppenhaus kann man Werke von Ross Bleckner und Andy Warhol bewundern.***

Chalet style with a difference: the bentwood chairs in the dining room were designed by Norman Cherner. ***Chaletstil einmal anders: Die Bugholzstühle im Esszimmer entwarf Norman Cherner.***

Festive mood in a contemporary setting: above the fireplace hangs a photographic work by Maris Embisicos. ***Festliche Stimmung in zeitgenössischem Ambiente: Über dem Kamin hängt eine Fotoarbeit von Maris Embisicos.***

The modern works in wood in the bedroom go well with Francesco Clemente's heads of "Ragazzo e ragazza". ***Zu den modernen Holzarbeiten im Schlafzimmer passen Francesco Clementes Köpfe von „Ragazzo e ragazza".***

Patina of three hundred years

A house is an extension of one's own personality," says Leonardo Mondadori. And because the Italian publisher is always on the lookout for the original, the natural, and is also passionately devoted to the inspiration gained from foreign travel, his farmhouse near Cortina d'Ampezzo, nearly three hundred years old, is "like a cocktail of different styles". For years the Milanese book expert had been searching for an old farmhouse in South Tyrol, the area where, since his childhood, he has most enjoyed relaxing and enjoying the mountain scenery. When his dream farmstead was offered to him, the Italian immediately recognized that this was the house he "had always had in mind", and that it possessed "the necessary natural qualities" that he longed for. Situated just outside Cortina in a broad meadow, the eighteenth-century stone-built house offers, besides a wonderful view of the Tofana mountain group, a most attractive interior. Leonardo Mondadori has furnished his mountain residence with original antique peasant furniture, and with charmingly unpretentious objects such as simple ceramic plates and wooden kitchen implements, which he combines with contemporary art by Robert Rauschenberg and Julian Schnabel. All this creates an atmospheric effect alongside the only lightly plastered stone walls on the ground floor and the rooms panelled with old wood on the upper stories. The renovation work took two years, supervised by Leonardo Mondadori working in cooperation with his interior architect Verde Visconti, a niece of the well-known Italian film director. It involved taking apart the whole house (which is under a preservation order), beam by beam, and putting it together again. "So everything is still original, the wood, the stone, the iron," says the Italian publisher, "except for the vegetable garden – that's new." Leonardo Mondadori loves his farmhouse – "now we even have chickens, turkeys and rabbits" – just as he does the surrounding landscape where he and his family like to spend time, only to return to a peaceful although unusual environment. For the Mondadori house has become a jewel: unpolished and yet brilliant at the same time.

Far left: the Mondadori family's guests sleep in antique, richly decorated beds. **Links außen: Die Gäste der Familie Mondadori schlafen in antiken, reich verzierten Betten.**

Left: South Tyrolean wood cupboard from the eighteenth century. **Links: südtiroler Holzschrank aus dem achtzehnten Jahrhundert.**

Top: The attic floor of this farmhouse near Cortina d'Ampezzo, owned by Leonardo Mondadori, gives the effect of a stage set. **Oben: Wie eine Kulisse wirkt der Dachstock im Bauernhaus von Leonardo Mondadori bei Cortina d'Ampezzo.**

Part of the hayloft was turned into a spacious party and function room. ***Aus einem Teil des Heubodens wurde ein geräumiger Party- und Gesellschaftsraum.***

Dreihundert Jahre Patina

Ein Haus ist die Verlängerung der eigenen Persönlichkeit", sagt Leonardo Mondadori. Und weil der italienische Verleger stets auf der Suche nach dem Ursprünglichen ist und sich auch leidenschaftlich gerne auf Reisen in ferne Länder inspirieren lässt, ist sein fast dreihundert Jahre altes Farmhaus bei Cortina d'Ampezzo „wie ein Cocktail aus verschiedenen Stilarten". Jahrelang suchte der in Mailand ansässige Bücherexperte nach einem alten Bauernhaus im Südtirol, wo er seit seiner Kindheit am liebsten ausspannt und die Berge genießt. Als ihm sein Traumgehöft angeboten wurde, erkannte der Italiener sofort, dass er genau dieses Haus „schon immer im Visier" hatte und es „das notwendige Urige" besaß, nach dem er sich sehnte. Etwas außerhalb von Cortina auf einer weiten Wiese gelegen, bietet das Steinhaus aus dem achtzehnten Jahrhundert neben einer wunderbaren Aussicht auf die Tofana-Berggruppe auch ein attraktives Inneres. Leonardo Mondadori hat sein Bergdomizil mit originalen antiken Bauernmöbeln eingerichtet, mit bestechend schlichten Gegenständen wie einfachen Keramik-

The bedroom is adorned by a fifteenth-century Gothic four-poster bed. ***Das Schlafzimmer schmückt ein gotisches Himmelbett aus dem fünfzehnten Jahrhundert.***

platten oder Holzgeräten aus der Küche dekoriert und mit zeitgenössischer Kunst von Robert Rauschenberg und Julian Schnabel kombiniert. All dies passt zu den nur leicht verputzten Steinwänden im Erdgeschoss und den mit altem Holz verkleideten Räumen in den oberen Stockwerken. Zwei Jahre dauerten die Renovierungsarbeiten, die Leonardo Mondadori in Zusammenarbeit mit seiner Innenarchitektin Verde Visconti, einer Nichte des bekannten italienischen Regisseurs, überwachte. Das gesamte unter Denkmalschutz stehende Haus wurde dabei – Balken für Balken – auseinander genommen und wieder zusammengesetzt. „Alles ist also immer noch ursprünglich, das Holz, die Steine, das Eisen", meint der italienische Verleger, „nur der Gemüsegarten, der ist neu". Leonardo Mondadori liebt sein bäuerliches Anwesen, genauso wie die umliegende Natur, in der er sich gemeinsam mit seiner Familie gerne aufhält, um dann schließlich zurückzukehren in ein friedvolles und doch ungewöhnliches Ambiente. Denn das Mondadori-Haus ist ein Juwel geworden: ungeschliffen und brilliant zugleich.

1680

Left: Costly woodwork in the bedroom. **Links: Kostbare Holzarbeiten im Schlafzimmer.**

A view of the parents' bedroom, with its en-suite bathroom. **Blick ins Elternschlafzimmer mit sich anschließender Badestube.**

Stilsicher

Der Name des Steinhauses „Chesa Val Suvretta“ stammt vom Engadiner Tal, in dem es inmitten einer Wiese voller Alpenblumen gleich neben einem kleinen Lärchenwald bescheiden, aber fest verankert in der Erde steht. Einst ein typisches Bauernhaus mit Erkern und Heuboden wurde es 1962 zu einem Berghaus mit elf Zimmern erweitert und einige Jahre später von Buxy Gancia mit viel Sinn für gelungene Kombinationen neu konzipiert und dekoriert. „Meine Wohnphilosophie lautet ganz einfach: das Innere eines Hauses mit dem Äußeren in Harmonie bringen“, erklärt die charmante Schweizerin, die St. Moritz und das Suvretta-Tal seit fünfundzwanzig Jahren zu ihrer Heimat erkoren hat, „also mische ich antike Engadinermöbel mit modernen Sitzgelegenheiten, starke Farben mit weichen Holztönen und rustikale Gegenstände mit zeitgenössischer Kunst.“ Buxy Gancia, selbst eine passionierte Malerin und Fotografin, hat ihr Engadiner Haus ganz eindeutig der Kunst gewidmet. Auf den weiß verputzten Wänden unter den Deckenbalken finden sich denn auch Bilder und Skulpturen renommierter Künstler wie Donald Judd, Jean Tinguely, Sigmar Polke, Joseph Kosuth, Gerhard Richter oder auch schwarzweiß-Werke des berühmten Engadiner Landschaftsfotografen Albert Steiner. Ein ganz besonderes Augenmerk verdient das farbenfrohe Doppelporträt der Hausherrin, das Andy Warhol, mit dem sie sehr befreundet war, 1968 vollendet hatte. Weil die Kunstliebhaberin gerne viel Platz um sich hat, hat sie aus vier kleinen Schlafzimmern einen großen Salon geschaffen, der gestützt wird von einem dicken, dreihundert Jahre alten geschnitzten Eichenbalken aus dem Tirol. Gleich zwei Kamine verbreiten in diesem lang gestreckten Wohnraum viel Wärme; darüber hinaus fällt das sorgsam zusammengesuchte rustikale Mobiliar ins Auge – antike Truhen, Schränke, „Gänterlis“ (hohe schmale Gläserbüfetts) und ein antiker, achteckiger Esstisch aus dem Berner Oberland. „Überall in meinem Hause verbindet sich Altes mit Modernem“, erläutert Buxy Gancia, die von ihren zahlreichen Reisen rund um den Erdball zudem eine abwechslungsreiche Keramiksammlung hinauf ins Engadin gebracht hat, „und ich bin überzeugt, dass diese Mischung stimmt.“ Wer würde es schon wagen, zu widersprechen – einer Frau, die einst bei Coco Chanel gelernt hat, was Stil, Klasse und guter Geschmack bedeuten.

***Oben:* Seit fünfundzwanzig Jahren ist die „Chesa Val Suvretta“ bei St. Moritz das Zuhause von Buxy Gancia.** *Top: The "Chesa Val Suvretta" at St Moritz has been Buxy Gancia's home for twenty-five years.*

***Rechts:* Moderne Kunst über einer antiken Holzbank.** *Right: Modern art above an antique wooden bench.*

ob·ject (ob′jikt; for v., əb-jekt′, ob-jekt′), n. [ME.;
ML. objectum, something thrown in the way; L.
objectus, a casting before, that which appears, orig.
pp. of objicere < ob- (see OB-) + jacere, to throw],
1. a thing that can be seen or touched; material thing.

A certain style

The name of the stone house "Chesa Val Suvretta" is derived from the Engadine valley, where it stands modestly but firmly anchored in the soil in the middle of a meadow full of Alpine flowers, just next to a little larch wood. Once a typical farmhouse with bay windows and hayloft, in 1962 it was extended to become a mountain home with eleven rooms, and a few years later it was redesigned and redecorated by Buxy Gancia, with a great sense of successful combinations. "My philosophy of living is quite simply to bring the interior of a house into harmony with the exterior," explains the charming Swiss woman who twenty-five years ago chose St Moritz and the Suvretta valley as her home. "So I mix antique Engadine furniture with modern seating, strong colours with soft wood tones and rustic objects with contemporary art." Buxy Gancia, herself a passionate painter and photographer, has quite single-mindedly dedicated her Engadine house to art. So, on the white plastered walls, below the ceiling beams, are paintings and sculptures by renowned artists such as Donald Judd, Jean Tinguely, Sigmar Polke, Joseph Kosuth, Gerhard Richter, as well as works in black and white by the famous Engadine landscape photographer Albert Steiner. Particular attention is due to the colourful double portrait of the mistress of the house, by her close friend Andy Warhol, which he completed in 1968. Because the art-loving owner likes to have a great deal of space around her, she has transformed four small bedrooms into a large salon, which is supported by a thick, three-hundred-year-old carved oak beam from the Tyrol. Two fireplaces ensure that plenty of heat is spread throughout this extended living room; what is also striking is the carefully selected rustic furniture – antique chests, cupboards, "Gänterlis" (tall, slender sideboards for glasses), and an antique octagonal dining table from the Bernese Oberland. "Everywhere in my house, the old is combined with the modern," explains Buxy Gancia, who has also brought a varied ceramic collection up to the Engadine from her many trips around the globe, "and I am convinced that this mixture works." And who would dare to contradict her – a woman who once learned the meaning of style, class and good taste from Coco Chanel.

Buxy Gancia kombiniert sehr geschickt moderne Kunst mit altem bäuerlichen Mobiliar. *Buxy Gancia likes to create very skilful combinations of modern art and old peasant furniture.*

Raritäten aus der Keramiksammlung der Hausherrin auf einem achteckigen Schiefertisch aus dem achtzehnten Jahrhundert – gefunden im Berner Oberland. *Rare items from the owner's ceramic collection on an octagonal slate table from the eighteenth century, found in the Bernese Oberland.*

Schwungvoll: Treppenhaus und Entree. Die Eingangstür stammt aus dem siebzehnten Jahrhundert. *Sweeping lines: the stairwell and entrance hall. The entrance door dates from the seventeenth century.*

A sense of tradition Traditionssinn

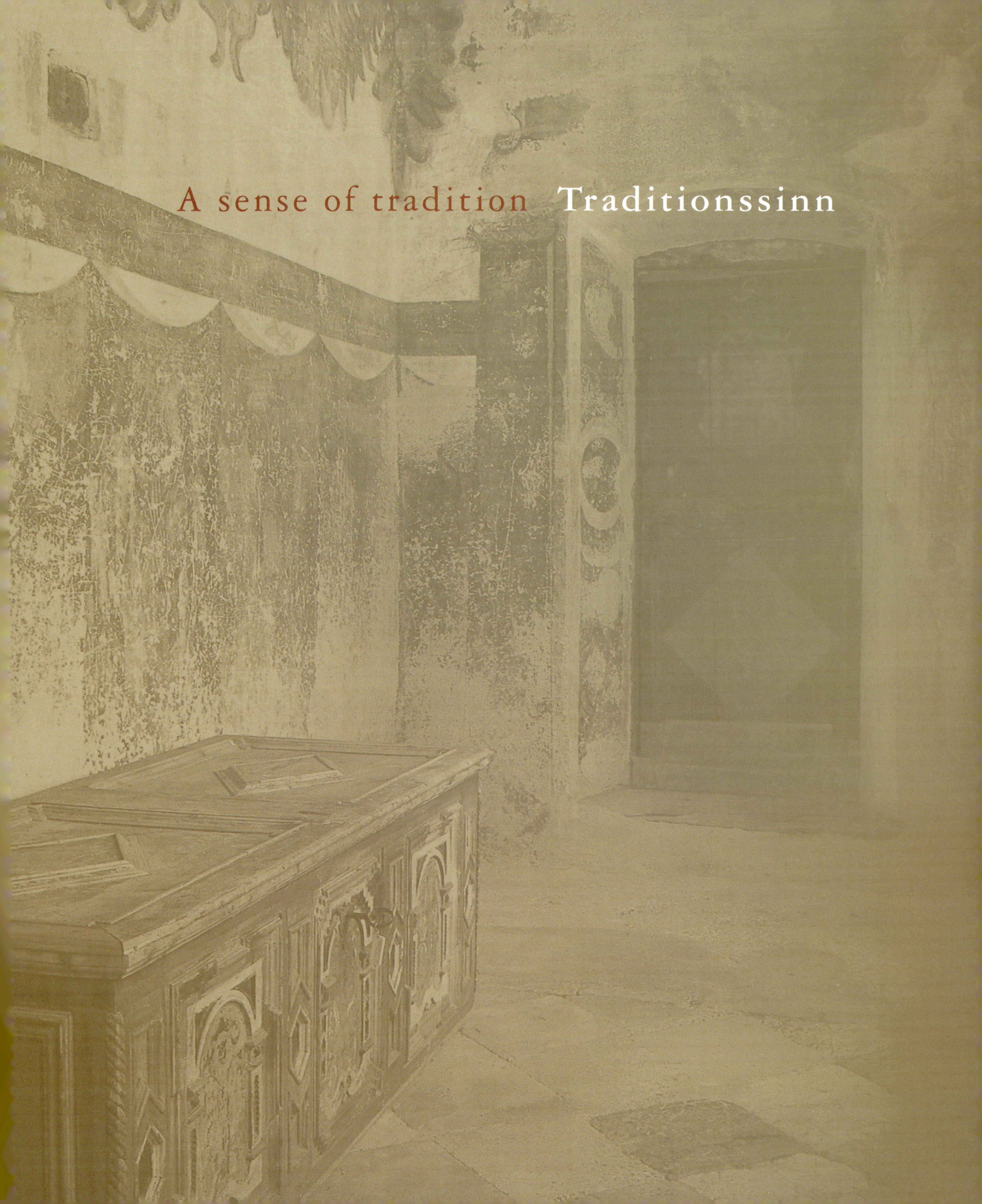

Alpine glamour

It has already lasted for thirty years – the relationship between the well-known pair of Canadian entrepreneurs and "their" Klosters. When it began, they had been looking for a place to relax, a place where skiing is more important than social obligations, and where, every year, there would quite definitely be plenty of fresh snow. And so they decided on Klosters, a village with a population of 3,700 in the canton of the Grisons. To this day the mistress of the house still enthuses over the efficiency of the Grisons builders, who in the early 1970s created a beautiful chalet with all its fixtures and fittings within only eight months. Today the house with the unusual name of "Viti Levu" (named after the main island of the Fiji Islands) no longer stands isolated on the hill with the splendid view of the Prättigau and of the Gotschna mountain opposite but is one of many attractive chalets that populate this favourite sunny slope. Yet it is still one of the most unusual houses on the Russna. This is certainly due to its owner, with her unerring eye for colours and fabrics. She wanted to furnish her "Viti Levu" in comfortable style, traditional on the one hand, but nevertheless eye-catchingly different – with a great deal of wood, but also with a number of colourful fabrics. "When the winter landscape outside looks so bright and white, it really has to be warm and cosy indoors," says the creative British-born mistress of the chalet, who, with her connoisseur's eye, also collects antique furniture from the sixteenth and seventeenth centuries, as well as exquisite paintings – old masters and Impressionists. In addition she had help with the decoration from her longstanding friend, the Canadian designer Robert Noakes, with whom she also designs her other houses around the world. And without Lenny Carter, the curtain specialist, who completed all the textile work at "Viti Levu" to perfection down to the last stitch, the owner "could simply not have realized some very sophisticated ideas". The woodwork is the responsibility of a Klosters man, Martin Zimmermann. Over many years he has been storing and conserving pine wood from old Prättigau farmhouses, two or three hundred years old, which had to be demolished. He used much of this wood in this house. Not only the floors, but also the panelled walls and ceilings, have been created from broad old wooden planks. Or, as in the living room, the coffered ceilings are made from old wood in imitation of the patrician houses at Fideris, a neighbouring village. But to give the old wood a really rustic touch, the well-known woodcarver Marco Walli, a Grisons resident, went to work in this chalet. He designed a tree of life for the ceiling of the small library next door to the salon, and for the top of the wall below he carved some inscriptions about books and the value of reading. Peasant proverbs adorn the beams in the bedrooms, various rosettes are to be found on the wooden columns in the built-in dining room, and the owners' initials are displayed, finely carved, above the old entrance gate

Far left: Impressive view from the Chalet "Viti Levu" in Klosters in the Swiss canton of the Grisons. ***Links außen: Imposanter Blick vom Chalet „Viti Levu" in Klosters im Schweizer Kanton Graubünden.***

Left: In the entrance hall, guests are greeted by the girl with the red hat by Harmen Willems Wieringa above an Austrian chest of 1737. ***Links: Im Entree begrüßt das Mädchen mit dem roten Hut von Harmen Willems Wieringa über einer österreichischen Truhe von 1737 die Gäste.***

On the sandstone fireplace, a seventeenth-century saint is enthroned among antique pewter jugs. ***Auf dem Sandsteinkamin thront eine Heiligenfigur aus dem siebzehnten Jahrhundert neben antiken Zinnkrügen.***

Glamouröse Gastlichkeit

Dreißig Jahre dauert sie bereit, die Beziehung zwischen dem bekannten kanadischen Unternehmerpaar und „ihrem" Klosters. Sie hatten sich damals einen Ort der Ruhe gesucht, einen Ort, wo Skifahren wichtiger ist als gesellschaftliche Verpflichtungen, und wo es ganz sicher alljährlich ausreichend Neuschnee gibt. Und so haben sie sich für Klosters entschieden. Noch heute schwärmt die Hausherrin von der Effizienz der Bündner Bauarbeiter, die Anfang der siebziger Jahre in nur acht Monaten ein fix und fertiges wunderschönes Chalet errichteten. Heute steht das Haus mit dem ungewöhnlichen Namen „Viti Levu" (benannt nach der Hauptinsel der Fidschi-Inseln) nicht mehr einsam auf dem Hügel mit der herrlichen Aussicht aufs Prättigau und dem gegenüberliegenden Gotschna. Heute ist es eines von vielen attraktiven Chalets, die diesen beliebten Sonnenhang bevölkern. Doch noch immer ist es eines der außergewöhnlichsten Häuser auf der „Russna". Das ist sicherlich der Bauherrin mit dem unbestechlichen Blick für Farben und Materialien zu verdanken. Gemütlich wollte sie ihr

„Viti Levu“ einrichten, traditionell einerseits, aber trotzdem auffällig anders. Mit viel Holz, aber auch mit vielen farbigen Stoffen. „Wenn die Landschaft draußen im Winter so hell und weiß erscheint, muss es hier drinnen erst recht warm und kuschelig sein“, meint die kreative Chalet-Herrin, die mit ihrem Kennerauge auch antike Möbel aus dem sechzehnten und siebzehnten Jahrhundert sowie exquisite Gemälde – alte Meister und Impressionisten – sammelt. Hilfe beim Dekorieren bekam die gebürtige

Left: Two steps lead from the bedroom into the little retreat with antique Swiss furniture, French chairs and an English sofa.
Links: Zwei Stufen führen vom Schlafzimmer ins kleine Refugium mit antiken Schweizer Möbeln, französischen Sesseln und einem englischen Sofa.

Top: Lenny Carter is responsible for the costly fabrics in the bedrooms. Here the choice was toile de Jouy by Braquenié.
Oben: Lenny Carter ist für die aufwendigen Stoffarbeiten im Schlafzimmer verantwortlich: Hier fiel die Wahl auf toile de Jouy von Braquenié.

Red and yellow on old wood: the Persian Ziegler Mahal carpet of 1880 goes well with the French, English and Swiss furniture of the seventeenth and eighteenth centuries.
Rot und gelb auf altem Holz: Der persische Ziegler Mahal-Teppich von 1880 passt gut zum französischen, englischen und Schweizer Mobiliar aus dem siebzehnten und achtzehnten Jahrhundert.

Engländerin zusätzlich von ihrem langjährigen Freund, dem kanadischen Designer Robert Noakes, mit dem sie auch ihre anderen Häuser rund um den Erdball einrichtet. Und ohne Lenny Carter, dem Spezialisten für Vorhänge, der alle Stoffarbeiten im Chalet „Viti Levu" bis auf den letzten Stich perfekt ausführte, hätte die Hausherrin zudem „manch raffinierte Idee einfach nicht realisiert". Für die Schreinerarbeiten ist der Klosterser Martin Zimmermann zuständig. Er hat über viele Jahre das Tannenholz von zwei- bis dreihundert Jahre alten Prättigauer Bauernhäusern, die abgerissen werden mussten, bei sich gelagert und konserviert und im Chalet „Viti Levu" vieles davon wieder verwendet. So sind nicht nur die Böden zusammengesetzt aus breiten alten Holzbohlen, sondern auch die Wandverkleidungen und Decken. Oder sie sind wie im Wohnzimmer aus altem Holz den „Kassettendecken" der Patrizierhäuser von Fideris, einem Nachbardorf, nachempfunden. Damit aber das alte Holz den richtigen rustikalen Touch bekommen konnte, ging in diesem Chalet der bekannte Bündner Schnitzer Marco Walli ans Werk. Einen Lebensbaum hat er für die Decke der kleinen Bibliothek neben dem Salon entworfen und für den Wandabschluss darunter einige Sprüche zum Wert des Lesens und der Bücher geschnitzt. Bauernweisheiten zieren Balken im Schlafzimmer, verschiedene Rosetten die Holzsäulen in der eingebauten Speise-„stube", und die Initialen der Hausbesitzer prangen fein geschnitzt über dem alten Eingangstor ...

This elegant dining corner was created from old wood by Martin Zimmermann; the paintings are by Maurice Utrillo and Marc Chagall (left). The labrador Motsko looks on admiringly. ***Aus altem Holz hat Martin Zimmermann diese elegante Essecke gezimmert; die Gemälde sind von Maurice Utrillo und Marc Chagall (links). Labrador „Motsko" staunt.***

Patio above the indoor pool with a view of the snow-covered "Hüreli" and the Davos mountains. ***Patio über dem Schwimmbad mit Aussicht auf das schneebedeckte „Hüreli" und die Davoser Berge.***

Old sandstone, old wood and old Swiss furniture give a countrified charm to the elegant pool extension. ***Alter Sandstein, altes Holz und alte Schweizer Möbel verleihen dem eleganten Poolanbau ländlichen Charme.***

Alpenburg im Südtirol

Sie ist eine bekannte Schönheit im Südtirol – Legenden und Historien ranken sich um ihre Mauern. Sie thront majestätisch auf einem Hügelvorsprung im italienischen Grödental (Val Gardena) gleich neben dem kleinen Bergdorf Selva. Ihre Außenansicht schmückt Postkarten, doch ihr Innenleben gibt sie nicht jedem preis. „Die ‚Fischburg' ist ein Privathaus und keine Touristenattraktion", meint der heutige Hausherr Barone Andrea Franchetti liebenswürdig, aber bestimmt, „unsere Familie wohnt hier in den Sommermonaten Juni und Juli – in der schönsten Zeit zum Bergsteigen." Die „Fischburg", die ihren Namen der seenreichen Umgebung verdankt, wurde in den Jahren 1616 bis 1628 als Jagdvilla im Renaissance-Stil erbaut. Der Auftraggeber war Edgar Wolkenstein, ein Nachfahre des im Spätmittelalter berühmt gewordenen Komponisten und Minnesängers Oswald von Wolkenstein. Das gleichnamige Dorf befindet sich denn auch ganz in der Nähe der „Fischburg" am Fuße des Sellastockes im Grödental. „Elgar Wolkenstein hatte sich damals für seine ‚Fischburg' vom Renaissance-Stil in der Toskana inspirieren lassen", erzählt Barone Franchetti, „er reiste herum und brachte seine architektonischen Vorstellungen in dieses abgelegene Südtiroler Tal." So ist eine für diese Gegend untypische imposante Burg entstanden, in der der damalige Hausherr zahlreiche Jagdgesellschaften bewirtete, zu eleganten Bällen lud und seine Kinder in den Sommermonaten mit der Welt der italienischen Alpen bekannt machte. Die nächsten Jahrhunderte überlebte die ehemals feudale „Fischburg" mehr schlecht als recht, bis im Jahr 1942 der Großvater des heutigen Besitzers, Carlo Franchetti, auf einer seiner Bergtouren im Grödental die verlotterte alte Burg entdeckte. Er erwarb das herrschaftliche Anwesen und begann langsam und mit äußerster Sorgfalt die zweiundzwanzig Räume des ehrwürdigen Hauses zu restaurieren. Die fehlenden Möbelstücke suchte er in den benachbarten Tälern wie dem Eschtal oder dem Sarltal. Seine Söhne führten die Renovierungsarbeiten weiter und suchten nach dem Krieg auch nach alten Tiroler Kachelöfen, die meist aus bekannten Manufakturen aus dem Val di Non stammen. „Heute besitzen wir mit über fünfundzwanzig Stück aus der Zeit von 1600 bis 1700 die wohl größte Sammlung Tiroler Öfen", erzählt Barone Andrea Franchetti, der zusammen mit seinem Onkel einige dieser Kachelöfen, die in unzählige Einzelteile zerlegt in den Kellern lagerten, „wie ein großes Puzzle" eigenhändig wieder zusammenbaute.

Seiteneingang in die Kapelle im Innern der „Fischburg".
Side entrance to the chapel within the "Fischburg".

Und auch er hat die großväterliche Suche nach passendem Mobiliar für die „Fischburg“ weitergeführt. „Es ist aber keine heroische Leistung, ein altes Schloss wieder herzurichten“, meint der in Rom lebende Hausherr schmunzelnd, „da gibt's keine große Konkurrenz, denn wer braucht heutzutage schon überdimensionale schwere alte Truhen und Schränke?“

Renaissance castle in the Italian Alps

She is a well-known beauty in the South Tyrol – legends and tales entwine around her walls. She is majestically enthroned on a hilly projection in the Italian Val Gardena, right next to the little mountain village of Selva. Her exterior is seen adorning postcards, but she does not reveal her private life to all. "The 'Fischburg' is a private house and not a tourist attraction," the present owner, Baron Andrea Franchetti, says gently but firmly. "Our family lives here during the summer months of June and July – the best time of year for mountain climbing." The "Fischburg", which owes its name to the many lakes in the area, was built as a hunting lodge in the Renaissance style between 1616 and 1628. The builder's client was Edgar Wolkenstein, a descendant of the composer and minnesinger Oswald von Wolkenstein, who became famous in the late Middle Ages. The village of the same name is quite close to the "Fischburg", at the foot of the Sellastock in Val Gardena. "Edgar Wolkenstein's ideas for the 'Fischburg' were inspired by the Renaissance style of Tuscany," Baron Franchetti relates. "He travelled around and brought his architectural designs to this remote valley in the South Tyrol." Thus, an impressive castle, untypical of this area, was created, where the owner of the time played host to innumerable hunting parties, issued invitations to elegant balls, and, during the summer months, introduced his children to the world of the Italian Alps. The once feudal "Fischburg" somehow or other survived the centuries that followed, until in 1942 Carlo Franchetti, the grandfather of the present owner, discovered the run-down old castle on one of his mountain tours in Val Gardena. He acquired the stately property, and slowly and with the greatest care began to restore the twenty-two rooms of this venerable house. He searched for missing pieces of furniture in the nearby valleys such as the Eschtal and the Sarltal. His sons continued his work of renovation, and after the war they also looked for old Tyrolean ceramic stoves, mostly from well-known factories from the Val di Non. "Today we have twenty-five examples from the period between 1600 and 1700, representing probably the largest collection of Tyrol stoves," says Baron Andrea Franchetti, who himself, together with his uncle, reassembled some of these ceramic ovens, which were stored in the cellars, dismantled into countless component parts, "like a huge jigsaw puzzle". And he has also continued his grandfather's search for appropriate furniture for the "Fischburg". "But it's not a heroic achievement, restoring an old castle," says the owner, who lives in Rome, with a smile. "There is not much competition, because who today needs oversize, heavy old chests and cupboards?"

Unter einem weißen Gewölbe speist die Familie an einem langen Holztisch mit passenden Stabellen-Stühlen. *Under a white vaulted ceiling, the family enjoys a meal at a long wooden table, with matching chairs.*

Perfekt proportioniert ist die Galerie aus Holz im ersten Innenhof der „Fischburg“. *This gallery in wood in the first inner courtyard of the "Fischburg" is perfectly proportioned.*

Rechts: Jeder Korridor eine Augenweide: Vor den bemalten Wänden stehen überall antike Truhen. *Right: Every corridor is a feast for the eyes: antique chests stand everywhere in front of the painted walls.*

Südtiroler Schätze: Wie dieses Schlafzimmer sind auch alle anderen Räume der Burg mit antikem Mobiliar eingerichtet, das aus der Umgebung stammt. *South Tyrolean treasures: this bedroom, like all the other rooms in the castle, is furnished with antique items of furniture from the surrounding area.*

Gotische Pracht: Dieses Zimmer hat Barone Franchetti einbauen lassen. Dazu gehört ein Tiroler Kachelofen aus dem siebzehnten Jahrhundert. *Gothic splendour: Barone Franchetti had this room specially built in. It contains a seventeenth-century Tyrolean ceramic stove.*

Nobility

Gstaad, the picturesque holiday resort in the Bernese Alps, is the home of Prince Vittorio Emanuele di Savoia and his wife Marina. Far away from the glamour of high society bustle, into which they also like to plunge from time to time, they take pleasure in their comfortable old wooden chalet, located outside the town on a solitary, broad meadow directly above a little mountain stream. The couple love their 1970s chalet, because the atmosphere in this house is on the one hand "cosy" – this is continually stressed – but on the other hand is also very individually matched to them and their family. And indeed, this direct descendant of the Italian King Umberto II surrounds himself in exile with so many family heirlooms that a visit to the Savoia household is equivalent to a lesson in Italian history. In the salon, in a built-in display case, hang the most charming picture frames, filled with a selection of miniature portraits of members of the Italian royal family. Old black and white family photographs in their chased silver frames are scattered throughout the house. With the help of the interior designer Claude Reyren, this prominent couple have had their chalet rebuilt and adapted to their requirements. "We wanted wood, wood and more wood," declares Princess Marina. And so the whole house was panelled with the two-hundred-year-old planks and beams that once graced a farmhouse in the area. When choosing fabrics, the designer and amateur decorator were equally uncompromising. The fabrics, almost exclusively from France, are delicately patterned, with beige as the basic colour. But without a doubt, the most spectacular room in the Savoia house is the guests' bathroom. The copper bathtub and all the other original accessories date from before the turn of the penultimate century. And to the delight of the guests, the bath water runs out of an old coffee machine …

Far from the bustle of society, outside Gstaad, lies the chalet of Prince Vittorio Emmanuele di Savoia. ***Abseits vom Societytrubel, außerhalb von Gstaad, liegt das Chalet von Prinz Vittorio Emanuele di Savoya.***

Family photographs of the former Italian royal family – decorative and eye-catching. ***Gekrönte Häupter: Familienfotos der einstigen italienischen Königsfamilie sind ein dekorativer Blickfang.***

Noble Herrschaft

Gstaad, der pittoreske Ferienort in den Berner Alpen, ist das Zuhause von Prinz Vittorio Emanuele di Savoya und seiner Frau Marina. Weit weg vom Glamour des High Society-Getümmels, in das sie sich zuweilen auch gerne stürzen, genießen sie ihr behagliches altes Holzchalet, das einsam außerhalb des Ortes auf einer weiten Weide direkt über einem kleinen Bergbach gelegen ist. Das Ehepaar liebt sein Chalet aus den siebziger Jahren, weil das Ambiente in diesem Haus einerseits „cosy" – dies wird immer wieder betont, – andererseits auch sehr individuell auf sie und ihre Familie abgestimmt ist. Und richtig, der direkte Nachfahre des italienischen Königs Umberto II., umgibt sich im Exil mit so vielen Familienpreziosen, dass ein Besuch im Hause Savoya schon fast dem Unterricht in italienischer Geschichte gleichkommt. Da hängen im Salon in einer eingebauten Vitrine aus altem Holz die hübschesten Bilderrahmen – angefüllt mit erlesenen Miniaturporträts von Mitgliedern der italienischen Königsfamilie. Alte schwarz-weiß Fotos stehen in ziselierten Silberrahmen überall im Hause verteilt. Mit der Hilfe von Interior-Designer Claude Reyren hat das prominente Ehepaar ihr Chalet umgebaut und ihren Ansprüchen angepasst. „Wir wollten Holz, Holz und noch einmal Holz", erzählt Prinzessin Marina. Und so wurde das ganze Haus mit über zweihundert Jahre alten Balken und Brettern, die einst ein Bauernhaus aus der Gegend zierten, verkleidet. Bei der Stoffwahl gingen Designer und Hobby-Einrichterin ebenfalls gradlinig ans Werk. Fein gemustert mit Beige als Grundfarbe sind die Stoffe, die fast ausschließlich aus Frankreich stammen. Der spektakulärste Raum im Hause Savoya ist aber zweifelsohne das Badezimmer für die Gäste. Aus der Zeit vor 1900 stammt die Kupferbadewanne und alle anderen originellen Accessoires. Und das Badewasser rinnt – zum Entzücken der Gäste – aus einer alten Kaffeemaschine ...

Top left: One wall is adorned by a seventeenth-century tapestry, the other by a pair of wooden skis from the 1930s. ***Oben links: Die eine Wand schmückt eine Tapisserie aus dem siebzehnten Jahrhundert, die andere ein paar Holzski aus den dreißiger Jahren des letzten Jahrhunderts.***

Top right: The high-ceilinged salon with its round bench in one corner is the ideal spot to meet friends. ***Oben rechts: Der hohe Salon mit seiner Rundbank in einer Ecke ist der ideale Ort für Begegnungen im Freundeskreis.***

Right: French fin de siècle, right out of a picture book: the copper bath for guests at the Savoia chalet. ***Rechts: französisches Fin de Siècle wie aus dem Bilderbuch: das Kupferbad für die Gäste im Savoya-Chalet.***

Badetraum Lakesite Dream

Wer Bootshaus hört, denkt meist an ein einfaches offenes Holzkonstrukt mit einem Steg und einem Platz für ein Boot. Doch dieses schlichte Bild hat mit dem Bootshaus von Sandra Skrein im Salzkammergut nicht das geringste gemein. Hier handelt es sich um eine Boots-„Villa“, und zwar um eine, die vom großen Berliner Architekten und Bauhaus-Begründer Walter Gropius in den zwanziger Jahren des letzten Jahrhunderts entworfen worden ist. Und dieser klaren Konstruktion hat nun Sandra Skrein mit viel Phantasie und ihrem gutem Auge für Verborgenes zu einem zeitgemäßen Aussehen verholfen. Aus einem ehemaligen Abstellraum hat sie einen herrlichen Aufenthaltsraum geschaffen – bestückt mit alten Liegestühlen aus Eiche und Korbsesseln aus der Zeit um 1900, die sie alle liebevoll restauriert hat. „Jedes Stück im Bootshaus haben wir aufbewahrt, selbst die Eissäge, die einst im Winter dazu diente, das Eis rund um das Bootshaus zu entfernen, aber auch die alten Bootsfender, die Fischerkörbe und antikes Angelzeug.“ Eine Rarität ist ganz sicher das alte Holzboot, das schon mehr als siebzig Jahre in diesem Bootsheim „wohnt“: Es wurde für den Mitbegründer der Salzburger Festspiele, Hugo von Hofmannsthal, gebaut ...

The word “boathouse” usually suggests a simple open wooden structure with a landing stage and room for a boat. But this modest image has not the slightest in common with Sandra Skrein’s boathouse in the Salzkammergut. This is more of a boat “villa”, in fact one that was designed in the 1920s by the great architect and founder of the Bauhaus, Walter Gropius. And with a great deal of imagination and a good eye for what is concealed, Sandra Skrein has given this straightforward structure a contemporary look. From a former storeroom, she has created a superb recreation room, equipped with old oak deckchairs and wicker chairs from around 1900, all of which she has lovingly restored. “We have kept every single piece from the boathouse,” reports the sportswoman, who sails or water-skis in the summer, “even the ice-saw which used to be used in winter to remove the ice around the boathouse, but also the old boat fenders, the fishing baskets and antique fishing gear.” Quite definitely a rarity is the old wooden boat that has “lived” here for more than seventy years: it was built for Hugo von Hofmannsthal, the co-founder of the Salzburg Festival.

Bühnenbild mit Wasser: Blick vom Badehaus auf den Wolfgangsee im Salzkammergut. *Stage set with water: view from the bathing-hut over the Wolfgangsee in the Salzkammergut.*

Bei einer Brise Seeluft lässt es sich unter dem Dach herrlich schlafen. *When the sea breezes blow, one can sleep soundly under the roof.*

Jeden Quadratmeter ihrer Boots-„Villa“ hat Sandra Skrein liebevoll dekoriert. _Sandra Skrein has lovingly decorated every square metre of her boat “villa”._

Vom Berliner Architekten und Bauhaus-Begründer Walter Gropius gebaut: das Bootshaus aus den zwanziger Jahren des letzten Jahrhunderts. _Built by the Berlin architect and Bauhaus founder Walter Gropius: the 1920s boathouse._

Sommerfrische

Ich hatte das große Glück, auf dem Land aufzuwachsen, und meine Eltern lebten uns Kindern dieses unverfälschte ländliche Dasein mit Leidenschaft und Hingabe vor", erzählt Sandra Skrein angeregt. Wenn man sie von ihrer Jugend mit den überwinterten „leicht schrumpeligen Jausen-Äpfeln", dem selbstgemachten Himbeer- oder Johannisbeersaft und dem Garten voller Buschbohnen, Tomaten und Kräuter erzählen hört, überrascht ihr eigenes Zuhause von heute keineswegs: Es ist ein verträumtes Jahrhundertwendehaus mit einem märchenhaften kunterbunten Garten hoch über einem See im Salzkammergut gelegen. „Eigentlich liebe ich schlichtes Design, die ‚Moderne' der dreißiger bis sechziger Jahre", erklärt die junge Frau, die sich heute ganz – privat und beruflich – ihrem „inspirierenden und aufregenden" Leben auf dem Lande widmet, „aber dieses Haus wollte seinen Stil selbst bestimmen – ein Zusammenspiel von Architektur, Einrichtung und ländlicher Umgebung." Konzipiert wurde die einladende Villa vom Prager Architekten Otokar Novotny, der wenige Jahre später den tschechischen Kubismus mitbegründete. Die gesamte Innenausstattung des Hauses wurde aber bereits in den dreißiger Jahren vollständig erneuert. Und mit der heutigen Besitzerin Sandra Skrein bekam das Haus schließlich seinen unvergleichlichen Stil. Die Lifestyle-Spezialistin, die Bücher zum Thema Haus und Garten verfasst und auf ihrer homepage dazu Tipps gibt, hat umgebaut, umgemalt, umgehängt, vergrößert, verbessert und neu verkleidet. Die hohe Halle mit den farbenfrohen Teppichen, den Sofas, den Beistelltischen und dem eingebauten Kamin, der an Wintertagen auch das Treppenhaus heizt, ist zu einem Salon geworden. Das ehemalige Speisezimmer, ein ganz in dunkel gebeiztem „Zirbenholz" ausgelegter Raum, hat Sandra mit Büchergestellen versehen lassen und zu einer Bibliothek-cum-Familienzimmer umgestaltet. „Hier haben wir auch unsere Sammlungen untergebracht", erzählt die Hausherrin, „in den Schaukästen finden sich die Modelleisenbahnen und -schiffe meines Mannes genauso wie meine Vasen, mein Porzellan und meine Keramik-Trouvaillen; die Gläser, das Besteck und die Tischwäsche, von denen ich nie genug haben kann, werden in diesem Haus aber auch so oft als möglich gebraucht." Die Küche wurde von Sandra Skrein völlig neu gestaltet und ist heute zum liebsten Aufenthaltsort der Familie geworden. Die Schlafzimmer in den beiden oberen Stockwerken bestechen durch ihre dunkle leichte Eleganz. Ganz schwarz gestrichen hat man eine neu eingebaute Vertäfelung in einem Schlafzimmer – einer Zeichnung von Josef Hoffmann, dem österreichischen Architekten und Mitbegründer der Wiener

Werkstätte, nachempfunden. Dazu passen die Leinenstoffe, die nach alten Mustern von Josef Frank bedruckt worden sind. Der österreichische Architekt entwarf diese Stoffkollektion mit Motiven aus der Natur bereits Anfang der dreißiger Jahre. Und so fügen sich Architektur, Farbe, Muster und Mobiliar zu einem harmonischen Ganzen, das zusammengehalten wird durch viele farbenfrohe typisch österreichische „Fleckerl"-Teppiche. „Diese Teppiche sind im ganzen Haus verteilt", erläutert Sandra Skrein, „sie sind aus alten Stoffresten von Hand gewoben, eben aus ‚Fleckerln', die wiederum von alter beschädigter Tischwäsche, von Betttüchern oder gar von Dirndlkleidern stammen – wir Österreicher finden für fast alles eine Verwendung, wir sind die Pioniere des Recyclinggedankens."

Summer Holidays

I had the great fortune to grow up in the country, and my parents – with passion and devotion – set an example to us children of this genuine country life," Sandra Skrein explains excitedly. When she talks about her childhood, with the overwintered "slightly shrivelled apples for snacks", the home-made raspberry or blackcurrant juice and the garden full of dwarf beans, tomatoes and herbs, her present home is by no means surprising: it is an idyllic turn-of-the-century house, situated high above a lake in the Salzkammergut. "Actually I like unpretentious design, the 'modern' style of the thirties to sixties," declares the young woman, who today dedicates herself entirely – personally and professionally – to her "inspiring and exciting" life in the country, "but this house had its own ideas about style – it demanded an interplay of architecture, furnishing and country environment." The inviting villa was designed by the Prague architect Otokar Novotny, who a few years later founded the Czech Cubist school. But in the 1930s, the entire interior decoration of the house was renewed. And with its new owner, Sandra Skrein, the house finally acquired its incomparable style. A lifestyle specialist herself, who writes books on the themes of house and garden, and gives tips on these on her homepage, she has rebuilt, repainted, refurnished, enlarged, improved and transformed. The high-ceilinged hall with the colourful carpets, the sofas, the side-tables, and the built-in fireplace, which on winter days also heats the stairwell, has become a salon. The former dining room, panelled entirely in dark-stained pine, has been provided with bookshelves and turned into a library-cum-family room. "This is where we have housed our collections," says Sandra, "and in the display cases you will see my husband's model engines and ships, as well as my vases, porcelain and ceramic finds; but the glasses, cutlery and table linen, of which I can never have enough, are used as often as possible in this house." Sandra Skrein completely redesigned the kitchen, and today it has become the favourite place for the family to gather. The bedrooms in the two upper floors enchant with their dark but easy elegance. A newly built-in panelling feature in a bedroom has been painted entirely black – inspired by a drawing by Josef Hoffmann, the Austrian architect and co-founder of the Wiener Werkstätte. The matching linens are printed after old patterns by Josef Frank, an Austrian architect who designed this fabric collection based on motifs from nature in the early 1930s. And thus architecture, colour, pattern and furniture come together in a harmonious whole, held together by a number of colourful, typically Austrian rag rugs. "These rugs are scattered throughout the house," Sandra Skrein explained, "they are hand-woven from old fragments of fabric, rags in fact, which themselves come from old damaged table linen, bedsheets or even dirndl dresses – we Austrians find a use for almost everything, we are the pioneers of the recycling movement."

Oben links:* *Das verwunschene Plätzchen mit Blick auf den Wolfgangsee verspricht Erholung pur. *Top left: This remote little spot with a view of the Wolfgangsee promises sheer rest and relaxation.*

Oben rechts:* *Einer „Sommervilla" aus dem Märchenbuch kommt das Jahrhundertwendehaus von Sandra Skrein sehr nahe; gebaut hat es der Prager Architekt Otokar Novotny. *Top right: Sandra Skrein's house comes very close to the idea of a summer villa in a fairytale; it was built at the turn of the twentieth century by the Prague architect Otokar Novotny.*

Österreichische „Sommerfrische": Zum Landleben gehören Dirndl, Schürzen und Lederhosen. *Austrian summer holidays: the dirndl dress, apron and lederhosen are all part of country life.*

Ganz im Stil von Josef Hoffmann ist das grüne Speisezimmer in der Skrein-Villa. *Quite in the style of Josef Hoffmann is this green dining room in the Skrein villa.*

Happy houseguests Logierlust

Hotel Ancora, Cortina d'Ampezzo

Certainly the most famous and most fashionable skiing oasis in Italy, with a population of 7,000, Cortina d'Ampezzo lies to the south-east of the Alps, quite near the Austrian border. Every year sees a pilgrimage of enthusiastic international celebrity skiers to this noble mountain spot, which has even acted as a backdrop for various Hollywood films. World-famous hit movies such as "The Pink Panther" with David Niven and Peter Sellers, "For Your Eyes Only" with Roger Moore as James Bond, and "Ash Wednesday" with Elizabeth Taylor and Henry Fonda, were filmed at Cortina d'Ampezzo. The centre of the renowned Olympic town, which can look back on more than a thousand years of history, is the pedestrian zone and the main street, the Corso d'Italia, in the middle of which is the historic church tower. And here, right next to the church, is one of Cortina's oldest hotels – the Hotel Ancora. This appealing house, with its wooden balconies, typical of the Ampezzo region, was built on the main square in 1826. With Venetian columns for the salons, Biedermeier style in honour of Emperor Franz Joseph for the "Terrazza Viennese", vaulted ceilings painted pale blue in the dining room, and a great deal of carved wood for the bedrooms – the Hotel Ancora is furnished as appropriate to its unique location in the South Tyrolean Dolomites: with Italian elegance and Austrian charm.

Sie ist sicher die mondänste und berühmteste Skioase Italiens, die 7000-Seelen-Gemeinde Cortina d'Ampezzo im Südosten der Alpen und ganz in der Nähe der österreichischen Grenze gelegen. Alljährlich pilgert eine begeisterte internationale Skiprominenz in diesen Bergort, der sogar in diversen Hollywood-Streifen als Kulisse diente. So sind die weltbekannten Filmerfolge wie „The Pink Panther" mit David Niven und Peter Sellers, „For Your Eyes Only" mit 007-Star Roger Moore oder auch „Ash Wednesday" mit Elizabeth Taylor und Henry Fonda in Cortina d'Ampezzo gedreht worden. Das Zentrum des renommierten Olympiastädtchens, das auf eine über tausendjährige Geschichte zurückblicken kann, ist die Fußgängerzone und die Hauptstraße, der Corso Italia, in deren Mitte der historische Kirchturm liegt. Und hier gleich neben der Kirche findet sich eines der ältesten Hotels von Cortina – das Hotel Ancora. 1826 wurde das sympathische Haus mit seinen für die Ampezzo-Region typischen hölzernen Balkonen am Hauptplatz errichtet. Venezianische Säulen für die Salons, Biedermeierstil zu Ehren von Kaiser Franz Joseph für die „Terrazza Viennese", hellblau getünchte Gewölbedecken im Speisesaal und viel geschnitztes Holz für die Schlafzimmer – das Hotel Ancora ist eingerichtet, wie es seine einmalige Lage in den Südtiroler Dolomiten erfordert: mit italienischer Grazie und österreichischem Charme.

Right in the centre of Cortina d'Ampezzo, on the Corso d'Italia, lies the charming Hotel Ancora, which was built in 1826. ***Direkt im Zentrum von Cortina d'Ampezzo am „Corso Italia" liegt das charmante Hotel Ancora, das 1826 gebaut wurde.***

Festive dining under the pale blue vaulted ceiling in the hotel's dining room. ***Festlich Tafeln unter hellblau bemaltem Gewölbe im Speisesaal des Hotels.***

South Tyrolean charm means carved and painted wood everywhere, including the comfortable bedrooms. ***Südtiroler Charme – sprich viel geschnitztes und bemaltes Holz – auch für die behaglichen Schlafzimmer.***

Hotel Chesa Grischuna, Klosters

Françoise Sagan hat hier gewohnt, die ehemalige holländische Königin Juliana, Paola von Belgien, Gene Kelly, Deborah Kerr, David Niven, Paul Newman, Mel Ferrer und Audrey Hepburn, Billy Wilder, Grace Kelly, und mit ihnen halb Hollywood. Die „Chesa Grischuna" an der Bahnhofstraße mitten in Klosters war vor fünfzig Jahren das Wintermekka der amerikanischen Filmwelt. Den Champagner in der schummerigen kleinen Bar im unteren Stock spendierte die Hollywood-Meute, den Kaviar – gleich büchsenweise – die griechische Reederclique, gesungen haben sie lautstark alle gemeinsam, und mittendrin amüsierten sich die einheimischen Skilehrer. All dies und viele andere wilde Parties und Festivitäten sind im dicken goldenen Gästebuch der „Chesa Grischuna", dem „Bündner Haus", fein säuberlich festgehalten. Gebaut wurde die „Chesa", wie sie in Klosters liebevoll genannt wird, im Jahr 1938 vom Zürcher Architekten Hermann Schneider, der auch die bekannte „Chesa Veglia" in St. Moritz entworfen hat. In Auftrag gegeben hatte sie der Klosterser Hotelier Hans Guler, in dessen Familienbesitz das wunderschöne Haus sich noch heute befindet. Als große Familie betrachteten sich die Gäste damals. Man kannte sich, denn man sah sich alljährlich, man mochte sich, denn man feierte einen Winter lang zusammen, und man respektierte sich, denn man teilte eine tiefe Leidenschaft für die Berge und den Wintersport. Heute ist es ruhiger geworden im Vierzig-Betten-Haus in Klosters. Die Außenfassade mit den Darstellungen des Bündner Künstlers Alois Carigiet ist zwar immer noch eine der schönsten im Dorf, das Restaurant immer noch das attraktivste, die Schlafzimmer immer noch behaglich ländlich und schlicht gehalten, die Bar immer noch ein beliebter Treffpunkt für Jung und Alt. Doch es fehlt Gene Kelly, der singend über die Holztischplatten steppt ...

Françoise Sagan lived here, and so did Juliana, former Queen of the Netherlands, Paola of Belgium, Gene Kelly, David Niven, Deborah Kerr, Paul Newman, Mel Ferrer and Audrey Hepburn, Billy Wilder, Grace Kelly, and half of Hollywood along with them. In the 1950s the "Chesa Grischuna", on Bahnhofstrasse in the centre of Klosters, was the winter mecca of the American film world. The champagne in the dimly lit little bar on the ground floor was provided by the Hollywood pack, the caviar – in quantity – by the Greek shipowners' clique, they all sang together at the top of their voices, and in the midst of all this the local ski instructors looked on with amusement. All this and many other wild parties and festivities are soberly recorded in the thick golden guest-book of the "Chesa Grischuna", the "Grisons house". The "Chesa", as it is affectionately known in Klosters, was built in 1938 by the Zurich architect Hermann Schneider, who also designed the well-known "Chesa Veglia" in St Moritz. It was commissioned by the Klosters hotelier Hans Guler, in whose family possession this lovely house remains today. A large family – this was how the guests saw themselves in those days. They all knew each other, for they met every year, they liked each other, for they spent the whole of their festive holidays together, and they respected each other, for they shared a deep passion for the mountains and for winter sport. Today things are quieter at the forty-bedroomed house in Klosters. The façade with works by the Grisons artist Alois Carigiet is indeed still one of the most beautiful in the village, the restaurant still the most attractive, the bedrooms still comfortably countrified and unpretentious, and the bar is still a popular meeting-place for young and old. But Gene Kelly is no longer to be seen singing and tap-dancing over the wooden table-tops ...

Rechts: Betont unprätentiös sind die völlig in Holz gekleideten Schlafzimmer. *Right: An unpretentious note is struck by the bedrooms which are entirely panelled in wood.*

Rechts außen: Stimmungsvoll ist diese urige Ecke im Restaurant. *Far right: This traditionally furnished corner in the restaurant is full of atmosphere.*

Das Mekka der Hollywood-Stars in den fünfziger Jahren war das Hotel Chesa Grischuna in Klosters, das im Jahr 1938 vom Zürcher Architekten Hermann Schneider entworfen und eingerichtet worden ist. *The mecca of Hollywood stars in the 1950s was the Hotel Chesa Grischuna in Klosters, designed and built in 1938 by the Zurich architect Hermann Schneider.*

Hotel Mont-Blanc, Megève

An hour from Geneva and only about thirty kilometres from the Italian border lies Megève, the little French alpine resort with its countless charming chalets, the stylish horse-drawn carriages, the traditional cobbled streets and the picturesque onion towers in the centre of this village with a population of 5,000. And in this town square, the Place de l'Église, tucked into an attractive row of houses, stands the Mont-Blanc, by profession a hotel, but rather a home from home. A few years ago, Jocelyne Sibuet and her husband Jean-Louis took over this chalet-hotel of around 1900, which although well known was rather run-down, and with wit and charm transformed it into an incomparably romantic holiday home. For this old house, in which Jean Cocteau, Charles Aznavour, Rita Hayworth and Prince Aly Khan once stayed, Jocelyne, a trained interior designer, searched for suitable fabrics – linen from Salzburg, Scottish tartans and floral material from the local Savoy area – and skilfully mixed their colours and patterns with antiques from Victorian England, local furniture and the decorative paraphernalia that really turns a house into a home. Today the Hotel Mont-Blanc in Megève, where prominent people such as the actress Jeanne Moreau, the socialite Nadine Rothschild and the fashion designers Hubert de Givenchy and Inès de la Fressange have holiday homes, has become the epitome of discriminating living at the highest level. On the way to Albertville, above a little meadow ledge, is a further find of the Sibuets', Les Fermes de Marie, which the couple from Megève named after their daughter Marie. It is a small group of farmhouses that together form one of the most unusual hotels in the whole Alpine region. It is Jean-Louis's passion to ride around the Savoy region looking out for disused old huts and traditional wooden houses which he then acquires, demolishes and rebuilds elsewhere, using the old materials to create a new structure. Nine simple huts, two to three hundred years old, form the basis for the enchanting hotel-village Les Fermes de Marie, where several buildings accommodate small guest suites, and others speciality restaurants, a beauty farm, a bar and an indoor swimming pool. What is especially captivating here is the love of detail that the creative couple have brought to the restoration work. Not only has Jean-Louis personally executed several of the many examples of woodwork and carving, but Jocelyne, too, demonstrates her many talents: quite apart from choosing the fabrics – often checked patterns by Ralph Lauren or KA International – and the interior as a whole, the committed hotelier's wife also painted some of the decorative pictures and designed the ceramic collection for Les Fermes de Marie. Also part of the Sibuet empire is the Hotel Au Coin du Feu, very near Rochebrune, which is much more reminiscent of a private chalet than an Alpine inn. No wonder, for here, too, the twenty-three rooms, the panelled sitting room with its large fireplace, the breakfast corner and the bar give the impression of a home from home. A successful concept which has become known beyond national borders, and one which Jocelyne and Jean-Louis Sibuet have finally used for their most recent Megève enterprise, the Lodge Park Hotel. This "hotel de charme" is entirely designed in the American trapper style, with a touch of the log cabin, from the bookshelves made from birch branches and chairs worked from elk horns to the thick checked woollen blankets for the built-in, cosy wooden bed.

Top left: A touch of the Savoy Alps, a dash of English country life. This is the style at Megève's prettiest village hotel. ***Oben links: Ein bisschen savoyische Alpen, ein bisschen englisches Landleben: Das ist der Stil im hübschesten Dorfhotel von Megève.***

Bottom left: Guests are welcomed with unmistakable charm at the hotel's reception desk. In the background, the passageway to the cosy breakfast room and the bedrooms on the first floor can be seen. ***Unten links: Mit unverwechselbarem Charme wird man an der Rezeption des Hotels empfangen. Im Hintergrund ist der Durchgang zum gemütlichen Frühstückszimmer und zu den Schlafzimmern im ersten Stock zu erkennen.***

Pinewood and tartan: the elegantly rustic salon at the Hotel Mont-Blanc in the main square of the village is a meeting-place for guests, and their guests, and their guests ... ***Fichtenholz und schottisches Karo: Der elegant-rustikale „Salon" des Hotels Mont-Blanc am Hauptplatz des Ortes ist Treffpunkt für Gäste und deren Gäste und deren Gäste ...***

A matter of attention to detail: here on the staircase, as throughout the Mont-Blanc, Jocelyne Sibuet has created a cosy feel, with antique paintings, figures and trophies. ***Es lebe die Nebensache: Jocelyne Sibuet hat jedes Eck – wie hier das Treppenhaus im „Mont-Blanc" – mit antiken Bildern, Figuren und Trophäen „heimelig" gestaltet.***

Just as comfortable as can be: a small bedroom at the hotel Au Coin du Feu, which, along with Les Fermes de Marie and Lodge Park, also belongs to the Sibuet empire in Megève. ***Einfach urgemütlich: ein kleines Schlafzimmer im Hotel „Au Coin du Feu", das mit „Les Fermes de Marie" und dem „Lodge Park" ebenfalls zum Sibuet-Reich in Megève gehört.***

Hotel Mont-Blanc, Megève

Eine Stunde von Genf und nur etwa dreißig Kilometer von der italienischen Grenze entfernt liegt Megève, das kleine französische Alpenmekka mit seinen unzähligen charmanten Chalets, den aparten Pferdekutschen, den urigen Pflastersteingassen und dem pittoresken Zwiebelturm in der Mitte des 5000-Seelen-Dorfes. Und an diesem Hauptplatz, dem Place de l'église, steht eingeklemmt in einer attraktiven Häuserzeile das „Mont-Blanc", seines Zeichens zwar ein Hotel, doch viel eher ist es ein Zuhause fern von Daheim. Jocelyne Sibuet und ihr Mann Jean-Louis haben das zwar bekannte, aber damals heruntergekommene Chalet-Hotel aus der Zeit um 1900 vor ein paar Jahren übernommen und mit Witz und Charme in ein unvergleichlich romantisches Feriendomizil umgewandelt. Für dieses alte Haus, in dem einst Jean Cocteau, Charles Aznavour, Rita Hayworth oder auch Prinz Ali Khan nächtigten, suchte die ausgebildete Interior-Designerin Jocelyne nach passenden Stoffen – Leinen aus Salzburg, Karostoffe aus Schottland oder Geblümtes aus der savoyischen Umgebung – und mischte deren Farben und Muster gekonnt mit Antiquitäten aus dem viktorianischen England, mit Möbeln aus der Gegend und dem dekorativen Schnickschnack, der ein Haus erst zu einem Zuhause werden lässt. Heute ist das „Mont-Blanc" in Megève, wo auch Prominente wie Schauspielerin Jeanne Moreau, Society-Dame Nadine de Rothschild oder die Modemacher Hubert de Givenchy und Inès de la Fressange ihr Ferienhaus haben, zum Inbegriff fürs Verwöhnen auf höchster Ebene geworden. Auf dem Weg Richtung Albertville oben auf einem kleinen Wiesenvorsprung findet sich eine weitere Sibuet-Trouvaille: „Les Fermes de Marie". Nach ihrer Tochter Marie hat das Megèver Ehepaar die kleine Ansammlung von Bauernhäusern genannt, die miteinander verbunden eines der ungewöhnlichsten Hotels in der gesamten Alpenregion sind. Jean-Louis Sibuet's Passion ist es nämlich, in Savoyen herumzufahren und nach verlassenen alten Hütten und traditionellen Holzhäusern Ausschau zu halten, die er dann erwirbt, bis auf die Grundmauern abtragen und in neuem Kleid aus alten Materialien an einem anderen Ort wieder auferstehen lässt. Neun einfache zwei- bis dreihundert Jahre alte Hütten bilden den Grundstock für das bezaubernde Hoteldorf „Les Fermes de Marie", wobei in einigen Häusern kleine Gästesuiten, in den anderen Spezialitätenrestaurants, eine Beauty Farm, eine Bar und ein Indoor Swimmingpool untergebracht sind. Was auch hier am meisten besticht, ist die Liebe zum Detail, mit der das kreative Ehepaar an die Restaurierung gegangen ist. Nicht nur hat Jean-Louis viele der zahlreichen Holzarbeiten und Schnitzereien persönlich ausgeführt, auch Jocelyne demonstriert ihre zahlreichen Talente: Von der Wahl der Stoffe – häufig Karos von „Ralph Lauren" oder „KA International" – und dem gesamten Interieur abgesehen, malte die engagierte Hoteliersfrau auch einige der dekorativen Bilder und entwarf die Keramikkollektion der „Fermes de Marie". Ebenfalls zum Sibuet-Reich gehört das Hotel „Au Coin du Feu", das ganz in der Nähe von Rochebrune thront und viel mehr einem privaten Chalet gleicht als einer alpinen Herberge. Kein Wunder, denn auch hier sind die dreiundzwanzig Zimmer, die getäfelte Stube mit dem großen Kamin, die Frühstücksecke und die Bar ausgestattet wie ein „home from home". Ihr gelungenes und mittlerweile über die Landesgrenzen hinaus bekanntes Konzept haben Jocelyne und Jean-Louis Sibuet schließlich für ihren – vorerst – letzten Megèver Streich, das „Lodge Park Hotel", angewendet. Dieses „Hotel de Charme" ist ganz im amerikanischen Trapperstil mit Blockhaus-Flair eingerichtet: vom Büchergestell aus Birkenästen, über Stühle gearbeitet aus Elchhorn bis zur dicken Karo-Wolldecke fürs eingebaute kuschelige Holzbett.

Styled consistently throughout but still individual: each of the bedrooms is differently furnished, but always with a love of colour and detail.
Durchgestylt und trotzdem individuell: Jedes Schlafzimmer ist unterschiedlich eingerichtet – aber stets mit Liebe zur Farbe und zum Detail.

Badrutt's Palace Hotel, St. Moritz

Von Friedrich Nietzsche bis Albert Einstein, von Alfred Hitchcock bis Vivien Leigh, von Thomas Mann bis Marcel Proust, von Alberto Giacometti bis Giovanni Segantini – selten ist ein einfaches Bergtal von so vielen brillanten Köpfen verehrt, beschrieben, gerühmt und in Wort oder Bild verewigt worden wie das Engadin im schweizerischen Kanton Graubünden. Seine große und illustre Gemeinde von Bewunderern kennt weder Landes-, Kultur- noch Altersgrenzen. Und St. Moritz, der Nobelkurort auf 1778 Metern über Meereshöhe gelegen, ist nicht nur Mittelpunkt dieses unvergleichlichen Tals, sondern nach eigenem Werbelogo auch gleich „top of the world". Gleichbedeutend mit St. Moritz ist das „Badrutt's Palace Hotel", die über hundert Jahre alte „Grande Dame" unter den zahlreichen berühmten Engadiner Hotels. Die Geschichte dieses Belle Époque-Palastes begann aber schon viel früher, und zwar im Jahr 1856, als Johannes Badrutt in St. Moritz die Zwölf-Betten-Pension „Faller" erwarb und sie zum Hotel „Engadiner Kulm" (dem heutigen „Kulm") ausbaute. Mit der Errichtung von Curlingbahnen und der ersten Rodelbahn der Welt „erfand" der St. Moritzer gleichzeitig den alpinen Wintertourismus. Acht Jahre später übernahm der Sohn von Johannes, Caspar Badrutt, das St. Moritzer Hotel „Beau Rivage" und ließ es 1892 von den bekannten Schweizer Architekten Alfred Chiodera und Theophil Tschudy zum Hotel „Palace" umbauen. Vier Jahre später wurde das weltberühmte Hotel, das bis heute im Besitz der Familie Badrutt geblieben ist, offiziell eröffnet. In den vielen Jahren traf das „Palace"-Hotel nur ein einziges Mal eine wirkliche Katastrophe, als nämlich der Turm, das legendäre Wahrzeichen des Jahrhundertwendebaus, durch einen Brand zerstört wurde. Heute steht das Prachthotel wieder in altem Glanz auf einem Grundstück von 23 000 Quadratmetern hoch über dem St. Moritzer See und ist unter dem Management der US-Luxushotelgruppe „Rosewood Hotels & Resorts" für die höchsten Ansprüche seiner prominenten Gästeschar ausgerüstet. Eine Hotellegende lebt weiter!

Die lange Bar im Restaurant „Le Relais", das europäische und asiatische Küche bietet, entstand unter dem „Rosewood" Hotelmanagement neu. *The long bar in the restaurant "Le Relais", which offers European and Asian cuisine, was refurbished by the "Rosewood" hotel management company.*

Links: Weltberühmt in St. Moritz ist das „Palace" mit seinem Turm, der 1967 einem Brand zum Opfer fiel und neu aufgebaut wurde. Das Hotel wurde 1896 eröffnet. *Left: World-famous – the "Palace" Hotel in St Moritz with its tower, which was destroyed by fire in 1967 and rebuilt. The hotel was opened in 1896.*

Badrutt's Palace Hotel, St Moritz

From Friedrich Nietzsche to Albert Einstein, from Alfred Hitchcock to Vivien Leigh, from Thomas Mann to Marcel Proust, from Alberto Giacometti to Giovanni Segantini – seldom has a simple mountain valley been admired, described, praised and immortalized in word or image by so many brilliant minds as the Engadine in the Swiss canton of the Grisons. Its great and illustrious community of admirers knows no boundaries of nation, culture or age. And St Moritz, the elegant health resort set at 1,778 metres above sea level, is not only the central point of this incomparable valley, but also, according to its own advertising slogan, "top of the world". Almost a synonym for St Moritz is Badrutt's Palace Hotel, at over a hundred years old the *grande dame* among the many famous Engadine hotels. The story of this belle époque mansion began much earlier, however, in 1856, when Johannes Badrutt acquired the twelve-bed Pension Faller and extended it to form the Hotel Engadiner Kulm (today simply "Kulm"). With the construction of curling rinks and the world's first toboggan run, the St Moritz hotelier at the same time "invented" the Alpine winter tourist industry. Eight years later Johannes's son, Caspar Badrutt, took over the St Moritz Hotel Beau Rivage and had it rebuilt in 1892 by the well-known Swiss architects Alfred Chiodera and Theophil Tschudy, when it became the "Palace". Four years later, the world-famous hotel, which is still in the possession of the Badrutt family, was officially opened. During all those years the Palace Hotel experienced only one major catastrophe, when the tower, the legendary landmark of fin-de-siècle architecture, was destroyed by fire. Today the magnificent hotel again stands in all its old glory on a site of 23,000 square metres, high above the St Moritz lake, under the management of the American luxury hotel group Rosewood Hotels and Resorts, and equipped to meet the highest demands of its many prominent guests. A hotel legend lives on!

Rechts oben: „Hirsch & Bedner Associates" aus Atlanta waren für die Neugestaltung des Hotels verantwortlich, so auch für die Einrichtung der luxuriösen Schlafzimmer. *Top right: "Hirsch and Bedner Associates" of Atlanta were responsible for the redesign of the hotel, as well as for the furnishing of the luxury bedrooms.*

Rechts unten: Die große Halle mit Blick in die Bibliothek ist ganz im Stil des „Belle Époque" gehalten. *Bottom right: The great hall, with its view into the library, is designed entirely in the style of the "belle époque".*

Dank

Mit jedem Buchprojekt sind Erlebnisse verbunden, an die man sich immer wieder gerne erinnert. Die vorangegangenen Seiten erzählen davon, von zahlreichen Begegnungen der ganz besonderen Art. Diese Begegnungen und die harmonische Zusammenarbeit mit kompetenten und liebenswerten Verlagskolleginnen haben uns einmal mehr viel Freude bereitet. Daher gilt unser Dank auch zuallererst den Menschen, die uns freundlicherweise die Türen zu ihren herrlichen Häusern und Wohnungen in den Bergen geöffnet haben, sowie den Damen des Nicolai Verlags. Darüber hinaus sind wir Inge Bienenstein dankbar, Rinaldo Menardi, Johanna Kothes, Evi Schmertzing und Elisabeth Thaussing, denn sie haben uns Kontakte vermittelt, ohne die das „Alpenbuch" nicht so vielseitig und attraktiv geworden wäre. Und zum Schluss gilt unser besonderer Dank Agi Simões, der erneut mit viel Feingefühl und Geduld die alpinen Domizile perfekt „erhellt" hat.

Acknowledgements

Every book project is bound up with experiences which one likes to recall again and again. The preceding pages tell the stories of a number of very special encounters. These encounters, and the harmonious co-operation with our efficient and charming colleagues at our publishing house, have given us once again much pleasure. This is why our gratitude goes out in the first instance to the people who were generous enough to open their doors to us at their splendid houses and homes in the mountains, but also to the ladies of Nicolai Verlag. In addition, we would like to thank Inge Bienenstein, Rinaldo Menardi, Johanna Kothes, Evi Schmertzing and Elisabeth Thaussing, who provided contacts for us without which our "Alps book" would not have been as varied and attractive. And finally, our special thanks go to Agi Simões, who has again perfectly "illuminated" the Alpine domiciles with great sensitivity and patience.

 Redaktion/Copy editor: Bettina Hüllen, Berlin/Laura Davey, Cambridge Übersetzung/Translation: Christine Shuttleworth, London Gestaltung/Layout: Pauline Schimmelpenninck, Berlin Satz und Lithos/Typsetting and lithography: Mega-Satz-Service, Berlin Druck/Printing: Aumüller KG, Regensburg Bindung/Binding: Kunst- und Verlagsbuchbinderei Leipzig Printed in Germany ISBN 3-87584-810-1